RUTH

RUTH

Road to Redemption

TERRI LUSTIG

Pleasant Word™
A Division of WinePress Group™

Pleasant Word (a division of WinePress Publishing, PO Box 428, Enumclaw, WA 98022) functions only as book publisher. As such, the ultimate design, content, editorial accuracy, and views expressed or implied in this work are those of the author.

ISBN 13: 978-1-4141-1368-5
ISBN 10: 1-4141-1368-4
Library of Congress Catalog Card Number: 2008911071

To those who are in the *highways* (Hod –os, in Greek, a road, progress, mode or means, journey, way)[1] and *hedges* (frag-mos, in Greek, a fence or enclosing barrier, partition),[2] those who are on the journey and hemmed in—that God's house may be filled. (Luke 14:16-24)

To all the Naomi's of the world—the abused, forsaken, hidden, discouraged, isolated, addicted, trapped and/or embittered—who may have lost their way. May you see with the eyes of your Redeemer and train to discern both good and evil.

CONTENTS

ACKNOWLEDGMENTS

I WOULD LIKE to thank Rita Baker, Nancy Ellis, Lori Fleming, Barbara Hogan, Cherie Seals, and Kathy Wagner for making valuable suggestions while studying Hosea, a difficult book to critique, which became the segue to **Ruth: Road to Redemption.**

I would also like to thank my husband, Keith Lustig, for reading my manuscript through twice, sharing great tips, studying the fine print for this contract, and supporting this project financially. I could not have done this without your blessing.

Additionally, I would like to thank Courtney McHugh, my future daughter-in-law, for your creativity and time spent developing my marketing materials, and to Tracy Snyder at Little Rascals Photography by Tracy in Mason, Ohio, for the great photo on the back cover of this book, and to the cover designers at Pleasant Word for the perfect cover.

Special thanks to my daughter, Laura Lustig, for reading through both manuscripts—**Hosea** and **Ruth: Road to Redemption**—and for writing the forward for this book. You are truly an inspiration to me—a woman who is full of faith in spite of the many famines in your life. You have chosen the narrow road, remaining in the place of training to discern, believing God for His blessings and inheritance.

Furthermore, I would like to thank Chuck Smith of Calvary Chapel, Costa Mesa, for introducing me to expository Bible study as a new Christian. Also, thanks go to Chuck Missler of Koinonia House for your superb teaching–line upon line, precept upon precept.

And finally, I would like to thank Adam Cothes for your positive response to my manuscript, George Dillaway for your commitment to excellence, and Mona Hodgson for a great editing job – all at Pleasant Word. I chose Pleasant Word because of your professionalism and great first impressions.

FOREWORD

AS A DEDICATED mother and an avid Berean of the scriptures, Terri Lustig has instilled in her children a love of the Bible from an early age. As the eldest of her four children, I can tell you that our mornings spent studying God's Word were some of the most memorable in my childhood. It was at the breakfast table each day, with Bible and concordance in hand, that I began to realize how awesome our Lord is and how much He loves me.

Sometimes it can be overwhelming to study the Bible, simply because you don't know how or where to begin. Believe me, I have been there. But I am excited to tell you that by opening this book, you are about to embark on a journey that is going to take you deeper into the scriptures in a way that will not only challenge your faith, but will also bring you encouragement and joy.

Mom taught me what it means to be a true student of The Word, and I hope that you too will find yourself committed to studying the Bible with a heart guided by the Holy Spirit. I can assure you that the passages in Ruth will come alive and minister to your spirit in ways you have never imagined. I pray that you will seek God each day as you open this book and pursue His heart through the book of Ruth. Whether you are facing a famine in your life, or know someone who is, may you find inspiration and redemption in the pages ahead.

—Laura Lustig

INTRODUCTION

I'LL NEVER FORGET the day I cried out to God to take me home to heaven. I was done here on earth. It took me nine long months to get to the place of surrender. Don't get me wrong…I would never take my own life, but I sure didn't want to remain on earth, watching my family suffer due to another person's sin.

I knew my cries were heard when the Lord gently spoke to me, "Good, you're right where I want you. Now I can live My life through you."

God's response brought peace to my heart that very instant. I began to realize that my life was not my own, and, that through much pain, the Lord had brought me to a place of total dependence upon Him. However, my cry of surrender was just the first step toward intimacy with Him—something my soul longed for. Now, you may be thinking that I had just said, "Yes" to the Lord for the first time; however, this was not the case.

I had made my official commitment to Him over thirty years prior to this experience and had given my life to Him over and over throughout the years. I had walked with Him with a great deal of resolve, following Him at whatever the cost, but this was different. Something had really changed! I knew my very survival was dependent upon my entering into His presence on a regular basis for the rest of my life.

My new journey began by a commitment to give up my cherished sleep so that I could spend time with the Lord every day. He was/is my bread—the sustenance of my life. I began to spend two hours a day praying and studying God's Word; asking Him to teach me His will and His ways; and learning how to hear His voice throughout the day and into the night. My dreams were becoming Heaven's pulpit filled with prayer strategies, teaching, and prayer burdens. The Word was coming alive and burning within my bones, demanding an outlet.

It wasn't a new thing for me to be a student of God's Word. I had a great introduction to studying the Bible as a baby Christian. I am grateful to God for placing me in a body of believers thirty plus years ago with leaders who taught the scriptures—line upon line, precept upon precept, from Genesis to Revelation. Back then, I can remember waiting in line to get into church; most believers were hungry for the Word of God. Sadly, however, some Christians today excuse their lack of Bible study for busy schedules, outward acts of religion, and for participating in programs developed inside the four walls of the church. Somehow doing outward *good works* seemingly have substituted intimacy with the Lord.

Church seems to be a place where we meet—instead of who we are. It is replacing the conviction of hearing the voice of the Lord as individuals to following after another person's agenda. This institution appears to be giving way to the dulling of a person's ability to embrace the Word of the kingdom and is minimizing one's purpose as something less than what God intended, which was/is to make disciples of all nations. This includes you and me. Don't get me wrong. I am not against the church—God's people; what I struggle with is the lulling to sleep of the body of Christ by replacing God's Word with itching ear messages which Timothy warned us about.

Preach the word; be instant in season, out of season; reprove, rebuke, exhort with all long-suffering and doctrine. For the time will come when they will not endure sound doctrine; but after their own lusts shall they heap to themselves teachers, having itching ears; And they shall turn away *their* ears from the truth, and shall be turned to fables.

—2 Timothy 4:2-4 KJVER

My transformation began over five years ago as a result of sin that was perpetrated against my family and me. However, the circumstances of our "famine" did not necessarily change. What changed was I learned to rely upon the Lord for everything. No longer was I a victim of my circumstances. I rose above them. I became a participant of the Word and began to realize who God is, who I am in Him, and that people are not my enemy. I learned how to see things from God's perspective and lay down the desire to get revenge or to exact full restitution, according to my own way.

My commitment to hearken diligently to the Lord has not stopped. No longer do I want to go to heaven as a copout for my pain. I awaken each morning excited about bringing heaven to earth as I wait upon God, praying and studying His Word. I am on the offensive as I hear what the Lord has to say about each situation. I am learning to discern both good and evil and have a confidence that whatever comes my way, God will give me the grace to overcome it.

Ruth: Road to Redemption is part of an ongoing series called *Trained to Discern* which focuses on why it is so important to hear the voice of the Lord while equipping you with tools on how to study the Word on a daily basis. Even though I have written three other Bible studies: Hosea, Song of Songs, and Esther (future releases), I have chosen *Ruth: Road to Redemption* as my first publication, because the Bible book Ruth consists of four chapters—a manageable portion for your success.

It is my desire to give you some learning tools so you can study the Bible for yourself and become dependent upon the Holy Spirit for truth. It is my prayer that you will branch off into your own Spirit-led study—gain knowledge, understanding, and wisdom, so that the Word is perfected in you.

This Bible study is different because I have written it in such a way that you will become an active participant—digging, listening, dialoguing, and applying what you have learned. You will gain confidence and have success so that your walk with the Lord will be on the offensive. The characters in the book of Ruth will come alive as you apply the spiritual truths you have gleaned. You will understand how to deal with life's trials through the lens of who God is and what your purpose is in Him. You will see some of the mistakes made by those who opted to take things into their own hands rather than remain in the "House of Bread."

Furthermore, you will observe the hand of God in the life of someone who had all odds against her. You will be confronted with famine, death, life-altering decisions and their consequences such as bitterness, a lack of hope, and an inability to see who God is in a life that is seemingly purposeless. You will be reminded of God's providence as He sets things right for those who place their trust in the One who can be trusted. Additionally, you will experience the grace, love, and the favor of God along with all the benefits associated with embracing your Redeemer, Jesus Christ.

Not only will you study the book of Ruth, but you will learn:

- Why you must nurture the Seed in your heart.
- What tools you need for proper growth.
- How you grow and what to do when your life seems over.
- Gardening tips.
- How to pull the whole study together with what you have learned through Orpah, Naomi, and Ruth.

All along the way, as you sample my harvest, you will have assistance from this gardener. So let's get started…happy gleaning!

Study to show yourself approved to God, a workman that needs not to be ashamed, rightly dividing the word of truth.

—2 Timothy 2:15 KJVER

Chapter 1

WHY NURTURE THE SEED?

AVE YOU NOTICED how hard it is to find a good church that teaches the Word of God and equips the saints to apply the Word and live it out in the marketplace? I find many churches are filled with mini-sermons devoid of messages on repentance, sin, and how to study the Bible for ourselves. In most cases, church is no longer a place where the saints are excited to hear the Word of God taught. Instead, church has become a social gathering, a business model, a place where our hard-earned dollars support buildings and salaries. Instead of being a refueling station for the perfecting of the saints, for the work of the ministry, for the edifying of the body of Christ (Ephesians 4:12), it has become a club house. But who said the church has the sole responsibility of discipling the believer?

Personal Discipleship →Disciple Others

Discipleship is the building up of the believers in faith. This should be the priority of all disciples. For when hard times come, the discipleship that has been nurtured will be the very fuel for survival. Our greatest witness comes when we live what the Word says in the darkness. The world can be a cruel place of existence with bombardments of ungodly acts from unrighteous people within the framework of unwelcomed circumstances. When we get to heaven, God will not hold the church accountable for the maturity of another individual; on the contrary, each believer will stand before God and give a personal account of what he/she did in Jesus Christ (2 Corinthians 5:10). And even though our personal commitment to discipleship does naturally benefit the lives of others, we are not responsible for anyone but ourselves.

The Ten Spies (Numbers 13-14)

Moses was told by God to send out men to search the land of Canaan. They were to see if the people were strong or weak, few or many; whether the land was good or bad, and if the land was suitable for crops and dwellings. Representatives were asked to bring back fruit from the land.

The spies returned with a branch holding one large cluster of grapes after forty days of exploration. The initial report was that the land flowed with milk and honey, but the people were strong and the cities were walled in. Most of the spies spoke of the various groups of people throughout the land and their concern for their obvious failure. However, Caleb silenced the people in front of Moses by stating that he was ready to go up immediately and occupy the land because he believed they were able to overcome all those obstacles (he was obviously a student of God's truth).

The other spies pronounced that they would not be able to go against the people because the "giants" in the land were stronger than them. How did they know that? They also shared an evil report about the land by stating that the earth devoured the people. Their report incited the people with loud wailings and murmurings toward Moses, wishing they had stayed in the land of Egypt to die there.

Thankfully, Joshua and Caleb spoke to the people about their experience in the land of Canaan—how it was exceedingly good. They believed the favor of God was on them, and that He would give the land to them. They admonished the people not to rebel against the Lord nor fear the people of the land. They believed their enemies were food for them, and that God would put them on the offensive and take away their enemies' ability to fight.

Unfortunately, it was because of the naysayers' unbelief and not listening to the voice of the Lord that kept most of them from entering into the Promised Land—even though they had seen God's miracles and knew of God's nature. It was Caleb, God's servant who fully followed God, and Joshua who were given permission to enter, along with their offspring, because they dared to believe who God was based upon what He did. Isn't this what we do when we study God's Word?

Notice Joshua and Caleb were responsible for their own entry into the Promised Land because of what they believed about God. The other spies received their due reward because of their bad report. However, the people were influenced by that bad report because they didn't know by firsthand experience. Each person was responsible for what they believed.

Personal discipleship is vital for recall of who God is and what He has done when the outcome means the difference between leaving our wilderness experience, crossing over the Jordan, and entering into the Promised Land. Personal discipleship begins with the individual and naturally branches out to all who will listen for the building up of the believers, or in this case, for the tearing down of them. Our beliefs greatly affect the lives of those around us when we vocalize God's truth and expose man's errors, but discipleship begins with the individual's obedience to the truth.

Bible Study →Think Biblically →Promote God's Kingdom

Our society has settled for a "separation of church and state" mentality to such a degree that the biblically minded are persecuted in most arenas. We are expected to think, believe, and act according to the mores of the culture rather than as ambassadors of a greater kingdom under the leadership of the King. As followers of Christ, we can influence our society for the kingdom of God, if we repent by thinking differently (Matthew 3:2). In other words, think the way God thinks. As we study the Word of God, we get the Lord's perspective on all issues pertaining to life so we can operate according to His will.

Thinking biblically can promote God's kingdom. Let us look at an example. After spending a great deal of time studying Esther, Ruth, Deborah, Rahab, and the Proverbs 31 wife, I am convinced that women have a destiny in God in all walks of life, just as men do. The Lord celebrates women throughout the Old and the New Testament. Recently, I received an e-mail that questioned Sarah Palin's pursuit of the second highest office in the land because it was "her job to be a stay-at-home mom." Whether you agree with this statement or not is not the issue. Our opinions do not matter.

In formulating the response to the e-mail, I found myself asking questions such as: What does the Word say about women in high office? Could Sarah Palin be a modern-day Esther or a Deborah? Is there a "carte blanche" answer? Can anyone speak for God in this matter? Just because we have been told that mothers belong in the home does not mean this statement is biblical.

After studying the kingdom of God twice, I noticed God's thinking is upside down and backwards as compared to how mankind thinks. I can think of a few examples: Hate is equated to murder. Lust is equated to adultery. When struck, turn the other cheek. Pray for our enemies. Family is equated to those who do the will of God. And Jesus speaks in parables, but tells His disciples they are to know the mysteries of the kingdom. According to culture, these statements do not make sense to the natural mind. However, in God's kingdom our first mandate from the Lord is to think the way He does. Therefore, our Bible study habits have the potential to make us think biblically, which should promote the kingdom of God.

The following scripture passage provides another example of the results of studying the Bible, thinking biblically, and promoting God's kingdom.

> For whosoever shall call upon the name of the Lord shall be saved. How then shall they call on Him in whom they have not believed? and how shall they believe in Him of whom they have not heard? and how shall they hear without a preacher? And how shall they preach, except they be sent? as it is written, How beautiful are the feet of them that preach the gospel of peace, and bring glad tidings of good things! But they have not all obeyed the gospel. For I-sa'iah says, Lord, who has believed our report. So then faith comes by hearing, and hearing by the word of God.
>
> —Romans 10:13-17 KJVER

Notice the result of calling upon the name of the Lord and being delivered was by hearing the truth from a person who obeyed the gospel and proclaimed the truth by faith. The Lord beautifully starts with the end result in this passage and works toward the beginning—the individual who has faith because of the hearing of the Word. So, we are to allow the Word to go into our hearts deeply so that our very words and actions line up with God's truth and build faith in the hearer; so that he/she can call out to the Lord for deliverance. This scenario begins with us. We cannot give what we do not have, and others cannot receive what is not given.

The Word Perfects Us

We need the Word actively working in our lives so that we are made into the image of Christ.

> Your word have I hidden in my heart, that I might not sin against you.
>
> —Psalm 119:11 KJVER

Your word is a lamp to my feet, and a light to my path.
—Psalm 119:105 KJVER

God's Word gives us the fuel needed to refrain from sin and follow His directives in our lives. It makes us free (John 8:32), cleanses us (Ephesians 5:26), teaches us to hear God's voice (Romans 10:17), divides between that which is of the soul and that which is of the spirit, and is a discerner of the thoughts and intents of the heart (Hebrews 4:12).

When we are attacked in our mind by the accuser of the brethren (Revelation 12:10) and we discern what is being said and who is saying it, we are "casting down imaginations, and every high thing that exalts itself against the knowledge of God, and bringing into captivity every thought to the obedience of Christ." (2 Corinthians 10:5-6 KJVER) We are to literally live our lives by every word that proceeds out of the mouth of God (Matthew 4:4, Deuteronomy 8:3) because the Word is living and powerful and does some deep cutting within the soul of man (Hebrews 4:12).

And finally, we are commanded to be doers of the word and not just hearers only, so that we do not deceive our own selves (James 1:22). This speaks of active study and personal application so that the Word completes the job in us.

Jesus, the Word – Our Example

When Jesus was led by the Spirit into the wilderness to be tempted of the devil after fasting for forty days, He was given the opportunity to succumb to the devil's "truth." However, Jesus used the Word of God as His weapon against the devil. Jesus believed that His food was God's Word—His power to silence the enemy and cause him to flee. He had to know the written Word in order to quote it, know how the Word was used in order to wield it, and know the power of the spoken Word in order to rebuke Satan. And after Jesus' ordeal, the angels came and ministered to Him (Matthew 4:1-11).

It isn't enough to nonchalantly read the Word whenever we feel like it. We are subject to violent attacks of the enemy that can threaten our commitment, faith, purpose, effectiveness in the marketplace, and our witness to those God places in our midst. Jesus' challenge had to do with who He is, what power He has, and what destiny He possesses. Are we not challenged with the very same things? God's Word must go deep so that we are not shaken by who we are, what our destiny is, and what power we possess in Christ.

God's Word Affects Others

In the previous story of the ten spies, the truth about who God is determined who entered the Promised Land and who did not. But the Word also affected what the others believed. The people had two choices: believe what the majority believed or believe what the two spies embraced. However, no one was without excuse because God's previous miracles spoke of who He is. So even though many did not have the opportunity to spy out the land for themselves, they still had the opportunity to believe the truth (Numbers 13-14).

We are admonished to be ready, always, to give an answer to every man that asks us for a reason for the hope that is in us (1 Peter 3:15). How can we do this if we lay down our only offensive weapon from God's provisional armor? When we pray the Word of God according to His will, we can have a part in eternity within the lives of those around us. Jesus prayed for those God had given Him before He was to be given over to His enemies for crucifixion. He asked God to sanctify them through His truth, His Word (John 17:17). He also prayed for those who would believe on Him through those who had already believed God's Word (John 17:20).

How important is our time in the Word if Jesus prayed for His current and future followers to be sanctified through the Word of God?

Jesus prayed for Peter after telling him that he would be sifted by Satan.

And the Lord said, Si'mon, Si'mon, behold, Sa'tan has desired to have you, that he may sift *you* as wheat: But I have prayed for you, that your faith fail not: and when you are converted, strengthen your brethren.

—Luke 22:31-32 KJVER

In both of these instances, Jesus' prayers had great effect in the lives of many—something that is immeasurable. Our proclamation of God's truth when we pray commands obedience.

So shall My word be that goes forth out of My mouth: it shall not return to Me void, but it shall accomplish that which I please, and it shall prosper *in the thing* whereto I sent it.

—Isaiah 55:11 KJVER

For Discernment/Protection

The only way to expose a counterfeit is to be intimately acquainted with the real thing. When I was working at the register in my first job at a fast-food restaurant, I was very familiar with how the paper money looked and felt. My boss had encouraged me to be very careful of fake bills, so I made a habit of flipping the bill over so I could see if the bill was tainted in any way. One day a man ordered food and handed me a $20 bill. I flipped it over and noticed that the front looked like the real bill but the back was a $1 bill. The thief had pasted four corners from four separate $20 bills onto the front of a $1 bill in the hopes of making a profit off the ignorance of his future victim, me, but I did not buy it. Because I had been trained in handling money, I caught the robber in the act and he fled the scene. In the same way, the more we study the Word, the more we are able to discern the counterfeit.

I have had numerous situations arise where I have had to expose error and confront sin. I am convinced that God uses those who are students of the Word in these types of situations so that His justice and righteousness can become the standard once again. After all, Satan does not make his tricks obvious; otherwise, Eve would not have been so easily convinced to bite into the fruit in the Garden of Eden (Genesis 3:1-6). God's Word was twisted just a little bit in order to cause her to sin, affecting all generations for eternity. If Eve had been a student of God's truth, she probably would have been more aware of the enemy's distortions and would have refused the temptation to sin.

Hearing the Voice of the Lord

> My sheep hear My voice, and I know them, and they follow Me.
> —John 10:27 KJVER

Hearing the voice of the Lord should be the norm. Since Jesus is the Word, it makes sense that studying the Word produces optimum hearing in regard to the voice of the Lord. We read previously that faith comes by hearing, and hearing by the Word of God (Romans 10:17). It starts with hearing the Word of God and understanding it, which leads to faith in action.

I have had so many instances where I have heard the Lord speak to me about a situation, person, or danger. Sometimes the Lord leads me into a situation because some clean-up work is necessary. There are other times when God wants to expose the heart and bring restoration to an individual. And finally, there are times when He just wants to teach me something.

One such incident occurred when I came to a small meeting for the first time. I was sitting in my seat, minding my own business, when the Lord allowed me to smell the scent of alcohol. Now, that scent was not a literal smell. No one smelled of alcohol. However, I was given insight about a particular gentleman in the audience who was struggling with alcoholism, and God wanted to set him free. I knew the Lord was prompting me to say something so the man would know God cared about him and could set him free.

I finally got the nerve to raise my hand and blurt out what the Lord had just shown me. I told the congregation the Lord had revealed to me that someone in the room was struggling with alcohol and was in need of deliverance. I knew who the man was because the Lord had told me, but I did not single him out in order to prevent him from any further embarrassment. The man leading the meeting did not even acknowledge what I had just said nor did anyone step forward in response to my seemingly ridiculous statements. So, there I sat, wondering if I had been out of line and should have kept my thoughts to myself.

The Lord prompted me a second time to speak out about what He had shown me. This time I waited until the leader was finished with the meeting. I raised my hand and asked if I was out of line or had missed it? The man who had the problem with alcohol sprang from his seat and said, "Boy, are you persistent! That person you were speaking about is me!"

Immediately, our small group gathered around the broken man. He raised his hands to heaven and cried out for help. I would never have experienced such joy and adulation toward my Heavenly Father if I had not heard His voice and responded in obedience to Him, even while looking so foolish. One sheep was apprehended by the True Shepherd that night as He showed him how far He would go to rescue His little lamb.

However, in case you are feeling a bit insecure about the topic of hearing the voice of the Lord, there was a time when I decided to wait on the Lord until He spoke to me. I went away to a remote place all alone. I sat on a large rock and waited and waited and waited…I was determined I wouldn't give up until I heard Him. After a very long time, I cried out to God in disappointment, "Why aren't you talking to me?"

In a still, small voice I heard, "I talk to you all the time, but you are not always listening." Imagine that. God truly does speak, but we are not always listening with spiritual ears.

And finally, I have not always succeeded in hearing the voice of the Lord or even heeding His voice when I hear it. There is always the temptation to hear it and then go about my way because the flesh begins to think it can do it on its own. This was the case one year ago when I began writing my Bible studies. I was inspired by a particular way of learning a subject and thought my Bible study would fit that pattern. Therefore, I would target a certain audience. One year later, after laying the Bible studies down for several months, becoming discouraged, and wanting to just quit (even though I knew I was supposed to write them), the Lord showed me I had heard His voice, but I was pursuing my own way. Now, I am back on track and have felt the anointing of the Holy Spirit as I write. So we can hear His voice, but choose not to heed Him because of personal pursuits.

Fruitfulness

It is an individual's sole responsibility to study God's Word and allow it to do what it was intended to do. With deep study come many benefits. A person who delights in the law of the Lord and meditates in it day and night is compared to a tree planted by the rivers of water and brings forth its fruit in its season; its leaf also shall not wither; and whatsoever he does shall prosper (Psalm 1:2-3). If the student allows the Word to germinate in the heart, fruitfulness will abound.

I liken us to a garden where God has chosen to place His most precious Seed—Jesus (1 Corinthians 3:9). After all, He tells us in Genesis that we are made in His image (Father, Son, and Holy Spirit). Each one of us has the potential to become what we were created to be. After all, His divine power has been given to us for all things that pertain to life and godliness, through the knowledge of Him who has called us to glory and virtue (2 Peter 1:3).

When we become *born again*, the seed that is planted in us breaks forth and it is up to us to allow the Holy Spirit to mature us in Him. Bible study is one of the major ways we can feed our spirit, not necessarily the activity itself, but the time invested in listening to the voice of the Lord as He teaches us all things (John 14:26).

Final Thoughts

In this chapter, we have learned that discipleship is nurturing the Seed in our own hearts so that eventually the Seed becomes a fruitful plant. In order for the soil of our hearts to remain soft, we must keep our hearts sharp for hearing. It is our responsibility to read, seek understanding, and apply the Word in all situations so that our roots go deeply. Tribulations and persecutions will come.

Our ability to apply the Word of God in all situations will only strengthen us for future encounters. Wielding the truth as a weapon can definitely protect us and bring discernment in our lives and the lives of those around us. We must think biblically. Think God's perspective—repent. Bible study is necessary for nurturing the Seed in our hearts. Fruit bearing happens when we hear the Word, understand it, and apply the Word in our lives.

In *Tools for Planting*, we will explore some of the tools used for tending a fruitful garden.

Chapter 2

TOOLS FOR PLANTING

THIS PAST SPRING I planted my first garden at our current residence. Our ground is made up of extremely hard clay, something definitely not conducive to planting a fruitful garden. In order to get the intended end result, I had seven yards of soil and compost delivered and dumped onto our driveway. My husband, son, and I took turns wheeling the soil from the driveway to the backyard, by alternating between two wheel barrows. Once the soil was in its proper place, I still thought it would be a good idea to rent a roto-tiller so the seeds would properly germinate. However, I did not heed those thoughts. Instead, I planted the seeds into the transplanted soil.

As I began to plant the seeds, I found it was hard to see where I should designate the straight rows because of the clumpy soil and where to place the seeds. I planted non-hybrid seeds (we will get to that later) hoping that after a successful harvest, I could collect the seeds for another year's harvest. I waited for several days and even weeks until I realized the seeds were not going to sprout. So, I went to several local nurseries and purchased "plugs" (seeds planted in a greenhouse, watered, and nurtured into small plants that can be transplanted into the soil when the ground is warm enough). So much for my own garden with limitless produce.

My garden had been reduced to a few types of vegetables because I did not prepare the soil properly.

Preparing the Heart – Using the Roto-tiller

My garden experience is a great place to start when talking about the heart in preparation for receiving the Word of the kingdom.

> Break up your fallow ground, and sow not among thorns. Circumcise yourselves to the LORD, and take away the foreskins of your heart.
> —Jeremiah 4:3-4 KJVER

> Sow to yourselves in righteousness, reap in mercy; break up your fallow ground: *for it is* time to seek the LORD, till He come and rain righteousness upon you. You have plowed wickedness, you have reaped iniquity; you have eaten the fruit of lies: because you did trust in your way, in the multitude of your mighty men.
> —Hosea 10:12-13 KJVER

These verses talk about the condition of the heart and its need to be softened. This prompts me to ask, "What does the roto-tiller represent in my own life?" First of all, I am to till my own heart, but to what end? The roto-tiller is to prepare my heart to receive the Lord.

This machine is whatever the Holy Spirit brings into our lives to prepare the way for the Lord. God will use anything to get us to a place of surrender. Earlier, you heard about my desperation, prompted by a traumatic situation in our family that caused me to want to cease my existence. God used that horrible situation to bring me to the point of greatest need—death to the flesh.

Hosea expressed the peoples' reliance upon themselves, trust in their own way, security in the multitudes of people, and confidence in their own strength—rather than in the Lord. Until I finally realized I could not work, earn, or prove anything in my flesh and that I was constantly trying to resurrect a dead corpse—instead of giving my flesh a proper burial so the Lord could live His life through me—I was telling God that His roto-tiller was not welcome. Why do you think there are so many self-help books available in the bookstores? It is more gratifying to the flesh to help it, rather than to yield to the Spirit of God.

If each person would begin their walk with the Lord by realizing that the flesh has died with Christ and welcome His resurrection power which dwells within, we wouldn't need a roto-tiller. However, I suspect that because we are human, God makes allowances for those times when we forget who we are by bringing the appropriate "roto-tiller" so we can die daily.

Any time we try to do something because it makes sense with the natural mind and then bypass what God is saying, we once again are in need of the roto-tiller. There are so many instances in the Bible where God does not make sense. Look at the many ways that Jesus healed people: He spit on eyes (Mark 8:23), rubbed another's with clay (John 9:6), and purposely waited until Lazarus died and stunk for four days before He healed him so many would believe (John 11:1-15).

In the Old Testament, Gideon's army was whittled down to three hundred people, and because of their obedience, their enemies turned on each other. One element that is not examined too often, however, is that Gideon's army had to break their own vessel and blow their trumpets in order to bring confusion into the enemy's camp—another indicator of personal roto-tilling (Judges 7:2-22). Joshua marched around the walls of Jericho seven times until the walls fell down (Joshua 6:1-20). Elijah was sent to be fed by the raven and then by the widow who had just enough oil and flour to feed herself and her son, temporarily. As she obeyed, the food supply continued to increase (1 Kings 17:6-16). In all of these situations, the natural mind was bypassed in order to obey the Lord.

> For My thoughts are not your thoughts, neither are your ways My ways, says the LORD. For as the heavens are higher than the earth,

so are My ways higher than your ways, and My thoughts than your thoughts.

—Isaiah 55:8-9 KJVER

The Parable of the Sower

Jesus taught many parables (hidden truths), pertaining to the kingdom of heaven. One of my favorite is the Parable of the Sower.

> Behold, a sower went forth to sow; And when he sowed, some seeds fell by the way side, and the fowls came and devoured them up: Some fell upon stony places, where they had not much earth: and immediately they sprung up, because they had no deepness of earth: And when the sun was up, they were scorched; and because they had no root, they withered away. And some fell among thorns; and the thorns sprung up, and choked them: But other fell into good ground, and brought forth fruit, some a hundredfold, some sixtyfold, some thirtyfold. Who has ears to hear, let him hear.

—Matthew 13:3-9 KJVER

Jesus further explains what this parable means—that it pertains to those who hear the Word of the kingdom. Some hear and do not understand, and Satan steals the Word that was sown in the person's heart. This is the first condition—the wayside. Some receive the seed with immediate joy but they have no root. They endure for a while, but when persecution and tribulation arises because of the Word he/she is offended. This is the second condition—the stony places. Some hear the Word and the cares of this world and the deceitfulness of riches choke the Word and the person becomes unfruitful. This is the third condition—thorny places. The final recipient receives the Word and understands it. This is the fourth condition—good ground (Matthew 13:19-23).

There is so much in this passage, but what I want to concentrate on is the only condition that produces fruit—the one that receives the Word and understands it. There are levels of fruitfulness accompanied with the fourth condition—hundredfold, sixtyfold, and thirtyfold. Therefore, the questions we must ask ourselves are: How do we foster the fourth condition so that we can produce that kind of fruit? What is the difference between those four conditions that enables a person to understand the Word?

The heart (soil) condition is the key. Fruitfulness comes when the heart is tended continuously. We must keep our hearts soft, pliable and open to the Lord's correction through His truth. It is not enough to hear the Word, but we must apply it to our lives. To whom much is given, much is required (Luke 12:48). We are responsible for allowing the Word to work the soil of our hearts to its fullest. The Word cannot be head knowledge but heart knowledge. It must change us.

Discipline – A Form of Tilling

In the context of tilling the soil of our hearts, Hebrews 12:1-2 talks about our need to lay aside every weight and sin which does so easily beset us, and let us run with patience the race set before us, looking to Jesus the author and finisher of our faith (Hebrews 12:1-2). One of the ways we can lay down our sin is to allow God to instruct, correct, and discipline us.

The book of Hebrews further talks about discipline and how we are to endure God's discipline so that we might be partakers of His holiness and yield the peaceable fruit of righteousness (Hebrews 12:5-11). Even Jesus learned obedience by the things that He had to suffer (Hebrews 5:8-9).

Discipline can be viewed through a negative lens, but in this case, it is training. It keeps us in a posture of submissiveness, humility, listening, and obedience. And if we endure His training, we will take on His attributes.

Root of Bitterness

We are also told in Hebrews to be careful of a root of bitterness.

Looking diligently lest any man fail of the grace of God; lest any root of bitterness springing up trouble *you*, and thereby many be defiled.

—Hebrews 12:15 KJVER

I have always focused on the bitterness part of this verse as getting rid of my own bitterness. This can be true. However, this is also talking about the root of another person's bitterness—someone who could defile many. The word bitterness here means to squeeze, seize, press, apprehend, take, and press down.[3] We must certainly examine our own hearts for bitterness, while apprehending any root of bitterness from the soil around us.

In the verses before and after, Hebrews talks about dealing with people and uses the example of Esau selling his birthright for a bowl of beans. Esau is described in this text as godless. He gave away his inheritance for his fleshly needs due to a severe famine. When you look at this admonition in light of how we deal with people and the fact that we are to watch the roots that appear in our soil, it is important to protect the heart and deal with those in our lives who may try to steal our water supply.

Discipline is not only for the individual, but for those around us. As we understand the Word, we are to speak truth into a person's life as the Holy Spirit leads, and hopefully, our obedience will lead others to true repentance.

Tools for Digging

I use a pair of gloves, a hand trowel, a small hand shovel, and a spongy pad for kneeling, while digging holes in the soil. After preparing the ground for planting, it is necessary to use the proper tools for digging the holes that house the seeds. For instance, I would not use a large shovel to dig a hole, because the seeds would go too far into the earth and become smothered by the soil. This would also prevent the sprouted seeds from surfacing because of the long distance between the soil floor and the sunlight. Nor would I use a dinner fork instead of a hand trowel to break up dirt clods for removing unwanted debris. Therefore, the tools we use must help protect the seed for optimum growth.

I find it fascinating that the Lord has created us in such a way that we cooperate with the Holy Spirit for our growth. He has given us a free will. There are things that we can do to maintain optimum seed germination in tandem with the Lord.

> So then neither is he that plants any thing, neither he that waters; but God that gives the increase. Now he that plants and he that waters are one: and every man shall receive his own reward according to his own labor. For we are laborers together with God: you are God's husbandry, you *are* God's building.
>
> —1 Corinthians 3:7-9 KJVER

The word husbandry in the text means garden, according to the secondary interpretation offered by the publisher. In other words, God is working inside of us and tending us from within to create a fruitful garden.

When Adam and Eve sinned by disobeying God's commandment not to eat of the tree in the Garden of Eden, they opened up a whole new kingdom of evil. Before that time, Adam and Eve had perfect fellowship with the Lord and were innocent before God and man. Satan had to disguise himself as a serpent with words of deception, and then once the lie was acted out, the gate was swung wide open to the demonic realm.

When Jesus came to this earth, His main purpose was to restore us to fellowship with the Father and place Satan and his demons under His feet and the feet of His followers. Unfortunately, many believers are unaware of the authority and power they have in Jesus Christ when it comes to demonic strongholds. Many leaders in the church have negated the role of the believer and even the power of the enemy. I find it interesting that in the Parable of the Sower, in each scenario, the seed was somehow stolen or an attempt was made to destroy the seed by the enemy.

The Lord's three-year ministry was made up of healing, teaching, and deliverance. We see many examples of people who were controlled by demons and in desperate need of deliverance. I have heard many minimize the believer's need to be rescued and find it ironic that those same people see evil permeate their own lives from generation to generation without understanding. I am puzzled with the ignorance of some when I think of Jesus' teachings on binding and loosing, the struggles we have in the mind and the examples that Jesus lived out so that His disciples could be made free.

If it were not for my own family having faced a traumatic situation, I may not have known what the enemy is capable of. Satan is bent upon killing, stealing, and destroying people. Even Jesus was confronted at His weakest moment, coming off of a forty day fast, by the devil and his minions. Why do you think the angels ministered to Him?

Demons need a wet place to live. It says in Matthew,

> When the unclean spirit is gone out of a man, he walks through dry places, seeking rest, and finds none. Then he says, I will return into my house from where I came out; and when he is come, he finds it empty, swept, and garnished. Then goes he, and takes with himself seven other spirits more wicked than himself, and they enter in and dwell there: and the last *state* of that man is worse than the first. Even so shall it be also to this wicked generation.
>
> —Matthew 12:43-45 KJVER

The demon came out and then returned. Have you ever wondered why the demons were able to re-enter? I have. Could it be that the person did not fill himself up with the fullness of God's Spirit? It says he was empty, swept, and garnished. There truly is a battle raging within each one of us because our ancestors from the beginning partook of the tree of the knowledge of good and evil. I believe the result of this decision is beautifully described by Paul and His struggle with the evil that dwells within him:

> For that which I do I allow not: for what I would, that do I not; but what I hate, that do I. If then I do that which I would not, I consent to the law that it is good. Now then it is no more I that do it, but sin that dwells in me. For I know that in me (that is, in my flesh,) dwells no good thing: for to will is present with me; but how to perform that which is good I find not. For the good that I would I do not: but the evil which I would not, that I do. Now if I do that I would not, it is no more I that do it, but sin that dwells in me. I find then a law, that, when I would do good, evil is present with me. For I delight in the law of God after the inward man: But I see another law in my members, warring against the law of my mind, and bringing me into captivity to the law of sin which is in my members. O wretched man that I am! who shall deliver me from the body of this death?
> —Romans 7:15-24 KJVER

Paul rightly instructs the believer about the evil that dwells within each of us, using himself as an example. Paul teaches further in Romans 8 about how to keep from walking according to the flesh by putting to death the deeds of the body through the Spirit. It is the Spirit of Him that raised up Jesus from the dead dwelling in us that makes our bodies alive and victorious over evil (Romans 8:11).

Hybrid or Non-Hybrid Seeds

Before closing our discussion on tools for planting, I think it is important that we talk about hybrid or non-hybrid seeds.

> Examine yourselves, whether you be in the faith; prove your own selves. Know you not your own selves, how that Je´sus Christ is in you, except you be reprobates?
> —2 Corinthians 13:5 KJVER

There are some who believe they are in the faith because they are doing religious activities such as: going to church, doing good deeds, reading the Bible, etc. Please do not misunderstand me when I speak of these things. These activities in and of themselves are not wrong; however, I am talking about doing these things as a substitute for the Lord Himself. There are others who may have responded to an appeal to be "born again" during an emotional moment but have not really changed from within. These types can be considered hybrids. Let me explain.

According to the dictionary, hybrid seeds are the result of cross-pollination between two different plants performing the same function—just as non-hybrid seeds come from the original plant without the cross-pollination of two different plants.[4] Therefore, a hybrid seed is a seed that is manufactured by man with an impure mixture.

Recently, I volunteered to participate in an evangelistic outreach. The six-day event was two-fold: training people to go out and "save" sinners and attending a nightly meeting to draw in would-be evangelists. However, I am getting ahead of myself. While attending the training, I wanted to leave because something did not feel right. As I walked out of the meeting during a break, I ran into someone I knew who encouraged me to stay. I was also asked by one of the leaders whether I was going to go out or not, and I vocalized my hesitation.

The young man convinced me that the nursing home would be the best outlet for me. I finally gave in and decided that maybe this experience would be a God-ordained experience. It was all right. As I walked into room after room, I was told to read a script and have the person(s) repeat the prayer after me. However, I was not allowed to give out any literature, have a lengthy discussion, nor do any follow up. The point of the exercise was to keep track of those who got "saved," regardless of whether the person was truly responding from the heart or not.

In one room in particular, there were four ladies. I could discern right away that one of the ladies was a lesbian. When I began to read the script, she immediately told me she did not want to hear it. The rest of the women followed her lead. However, the "trainer" proceeded to tell me to read the script anyway. I continued reading the script against my will and the will of those women. When I finally was able to walk out of the room, the trainer told me that while I was reading the script, some of the ladies were moving their lips, so to go ahead and put the tallies on the record sheet, signifying more people prayed the sinner's prayer and were born again.

That experience only forced me to get into the Word of God when I got home that day. I poured over the scriptures about salvation, being born again, eternal life, etc. It only made me hungrier for the truth of the gospel—not for man's ways of manipulation. When I prayed to the Lord about this situation, He told me that man had reduced His plan of redemption to "spiritual cloning." Ouch! I wanted no part of that.

So, in keeping with the theme of tilling the soil of our hearts, it is never too late to repent and ask God to break open the true Seed that has been placed in you. Refuse the hybrid seed that the enemy has tried to manufacture such as religion and traditions of men, saying an emotional prayer without full commitment and any other shortcut or man-induced substitute.

Final Thoughts

In *Tools for Planting*, we have explored how important it is to prepare the soil of our hearts properly, the tools needed for breaking up the soil such as: discipline, the eradication of bitterness and all kinds of evil. We also learned that the only type of seed that should be nurtured in our hearts is the pure Word of the Kingdom. However, there are more elements needed to maintain a garden than just preparing the soil.

In the next chapter, *How We Grow*, we will look at what the Seed needs for optimum growth.

Chapter 3

HOW WE GROW

I LOVE THE way God uses everyday events as object lessons. Just as the farmer plants the seeds and waits for the sprouts to pop up from the ground, so must we wait to see what God does in us. Sometimes we see immediate results and other times, it almost feels like we are taken around the same bush several times until we get it right. In this chapter, we will discuss the elements needed to grow into a mature plant. We have already discussed the need to die to self and dig out roots that steal water, nurture only non-hybrid seeds and dig out any debris. Now we will observe what happens above the soil once the seed has entered the ground.

Water

First and foremost, seeds demand water for sprouting. You can have the perfect soil and enough light, but if there is no water, the seed will not sprout. Have you ever done an experiment with lima beans using a baby food jar, a wet piece of paper towel, and watched a bean sprout? You will not see the seed break forth until the water is applied to the paper towel wedged against the bean next to the side of the jar. It is fun watching how long the bean takes to burst forth and in what direction it sprouts, moment by moment, day by day. In the same way we need water, we need the Holy Spirit to cause us to grow.

Furthermore, we do not need a teacher to teach us the Word of God. If you are a believer, you have the Holy Spirit inside you, whose job it is to teach you all things. In 1 John 2, John talks about many antichrists who were at one point part of the fellowship of believers, but had left the flock. He said the believers have an unction from the Holy One.

> But you have an unction from the Holy One, and you know all things.
> —1 John 2:20 KJVER

> But the anointing which you have received of Him abides in you, and you need not that any man teach you: but as the same anointing teaches you of all things, and is truth, and is no lie, and even as it has taught you, you shall abide in Him.
> —1 John 2:27 KJVER

These verses speak of the Holy Spirit being your teacher as you remain in Him. However, this does not negate the blessings of being taught by others. It just means that we each are to be taught of the Lord first and foremost.

The ones who left the fellowship of the believers were called antichrists—opponents of the Messiah (Anointed One).[5] It is vital that we remain in Him to guard against fighting against the anointing. This is why we need to be in a constant attitude of repentance. This process works in tandem. As we go into the ground (die to self) and receive the water (Holy Spirit) into our lives, we assist in our growth.

The scriptures admonish us to be filled with the Holy Spirit (Ephesians 5:18). The word *be* in this passage means to be being filled—a present, continuous action. The only way we can be continuously and totally filled with the Holy Spirit is to empty ourselves of the things of the flesh and welcome the Holy Spirit. This is where the anointing comes in: The Holy Spirit speaks about an area of sin, conviction takes hold, repentance is enacted, and growth follows.

Nutrients

It was my original intent to roto-till my clay soil. However, after reading materials on gardening, I realized that the soil needed to be 'prepared'. I found out there are tests to be taken that can actually measure how alkaline the soil is so nutrients can be added to replace the deficiencies. Rather than go that route, I opted to carry in new soil along with compost and add some fertilizer at various intervals. Nonetheless, I knew I needed to do something and just adding more "goodies" was the way to go. The woman at the nursery also told me I could lay newspaper down on top of the clay and start over. That sounded easy, so that is what I did.

In keeping with the theme, nutrients represent food—that which is ingested. Have you heard the saying, "garbage in, garbage out?" Well, the same can be true of nutrients in, nutrients out. It really does matter what we feed ourselves. If we live on a steady diet of TV, entertainment, gossip, or violent movies, we can be sure that our time in the Word of God and any subsequent understanding has a potential to be blocked, after engaging in such activities. And, in the same way, keeping a steady flow of spiritual vitamins keeps the spirit-man attuned to the things of the Spirit. Now, I am not talking about physical food but spiritual.

Jesus talks about the things we ingest in the book of Matthew. He addresses the scribes and Pharisees and confronts their hypocrisy.

> This people draw near to Me with their mouth, and honor Me with their lips; but their heart is far from Me. But in vain they do worship Me, teaching for doctrines the commandments of men. And He called the multitude, and said to them, Hear, and understand: Not that which goes into the mouth defiles a man; but that which comes out of the mouth, this defiles a man.
>
> —Matthew 15:8-11 KJVER

And Je´sus said, Are you also yet without understanding? Do not you yet understand, that whatsoever enters in at the mouth goes into the belly, and is cast out into the draught? But those things which proceed out of the mouth come forth from the heart; and they defile the man. For out of the heart proceed evil thoughts, murders, adulteries, fornications, thefts, false witness, blasphemies: These are the things which defile a man: but to eat with unwashed hands defiles not a man.

—Matthew 15:16-20 KJVER

Jesus is talking about spiritual food, using an interplay of physical food. He is making it clear that what a person takes in spiritually (in this case in a negative sense) comes out of the heart and becomes vile. He is also addressing the fact that the scribes and Pharisees felt clean because they were doing all the right things (outwardly), but their hearts (inwardly) were far from God.

I think it is interesting that Jesus refers to food as doing the will of Him that sent Me; to finish His work (John 4:34). He tells the disciples in this passage that He has meat that they are not aware of. This is because they were more concerned about Jesus' physical needs—whether He had food for the body or not. Jesus stresses how much more important His spiritual food is, and so should we. Therefore, we must protect our spiritual eyes and ear gates from that which can harm us. The question each of us should ask ourselves is: Will this "food" further God's kingdom or defile myself and others?

Light

Light has many connotations; however, we are going to look at light as that which illumines our ability to see and comprehend what God is saying.

This then is the message which we have heard of Him, and declare to you, that God is light, and in Him is no darkness at all. If we say that we have fellowship with Him, and walk in darkness, we lie, and do not the truth: But if we walk in the light, as He is in the light, we have fellowship one with another, and the blood of Je´sus Christ His Son cleanses us from all sin.

—1 John 1:5-7 KJVER

The point of this passage is that we cannot have fellowship with the Lord if we are not honest with our spiritual condition. The Holy Spirit's job is to convict us of sin. He is very good at shining a flashlight at our weaknesses so that we can be in a constant state of fellowship with Him. We need the light so we can be honest with ourselves and God.

Constant fellowship with the Lord is necessary to stay in the light, otherwise, Bible study can be just another activity. Fellowship is a two-way communication between God and man. There are times when something is not obvious, and in those times we are to seek the Lord until we receive an answer. One such time occurred for me one morning. The Lord had given me a word in my sleep and I knew I was to investigate the meaning. It was really strange because I did not even know how to pronounce the word, much less define it.

The word sounded like *messozini*. I spent that morning typing different versions of the word on the Internet and looking for possible meanings. The Lord had not even given me a subject or a clue, all I knew was that He wanted to teach me something about this word. I contacted some of my friends, asking if they had heard of the word. I even asked my sister who prided herself with a strong vocabulary by doing daily crossword puzzles, and she did not know.

Within a couple of days, I heard the word used in a sentence and recognized it. "Misogyny," I proclaimed. Then I asked what it meant. My friend responded with the meaning, "hatred of women!" Wow! It just so happened (there is no such thing as a coincidence in God's kingdom) that I was put in a situation that warranted the meaning of this word. The Lord was showing me prayer strategies, beginning with the understanding of the spirit of misogyny operating in people around me.

There are times when the Holy Spirit will lead me into a fast of some sort. I cannot say that I have always fully understood why I should fast. However, after studying the red-letter scriptures pertaining to the kingdom of God, I am convinced that fasting is another way to get the Lord's perspective on a matter.

> From that time Je′sus began to preach, and to say, Repent: for the kingdom of heaven is at hand.
> —Matthew 4:17 KJVER

In the context of Jesus' words, the word *repent* means to think differently, reconsider.[6] So as I change my thinking to line up with God's thinking, I am ushering in the kingdom of God.

> But you, when you fast, anoint your head, and wash your face.
> —Matthew 6:17 KJVER

I studied the words used in this passage and found that *anoint the head* means to oil with perfume and seize the head. And *wash the face* means to cleanse the view.[7] In other words, when we fast, we are literally putting ourselves in a position to change our thinking and see things from God's perspective. It takes great discipline to refrain from thinking through the lens of the intellect rather than through the light of God's truth.

Fencing

My husband, son, and I lugged heavy timber over to the new garden plot. According to the home owner's agreement, the garden could be three hundred square feet. With the added soil and compost, we decided to make a neat, upraised garden by strategically placing the timber around the designated plot. The final touches brought metal posts and a wire fencing to keep out unwanted visitors.

I learned that if I planted certain plants in the garden, I could attract the right kind of insects. So, not only was I concerned with keeping the thieves out, but I also welcomed those insects that would eat the pesky critters who would poke holes in certain vegetables. In the same way, in order to protect the Seed within us, we must be careful who we allow in our lives. Just as TV, scary movies, and too much entertainment can snuff out the spiritual progress of the believer, there are some barriers that are needed to keep out those who would sabotage God's purposes in our lives.

> Put on the whole armor of God, that you may be able to stand against the wiles of the devil. For we wrestle not against flesh and blood, but against principalities, against powers, against the rulers of the darkness of this world, against spiritual wickedness in high *places.*
> —Ephesians 6:11-12 KJVER

People are not our enemy, but Satan uses people to further his evil plans. The best way to stunt a person's growth is to allow Satan to manipulate people. If he cannot steal the seed through trials, persecution, distractions, and the ilk, he will certainly try stunting a person's growth through the offenses of others.

I have done an extensive study on forgiveness, true repentance, and restoration. I believe these principles have been misinterpreted to the point where believers are stuck in relationships that are unhealthy. I believe we are to confront sin in humility. However, if a person continues to sin, there comes a point when a person must separate from the relationship until there is true repentance, especially if the relationship is hindering the Lord's work. Of course, this would be the time to truly seek the Lord for His perspective through prayer and fasting.

Weeding

My intentions were good, my plans grandiose, but little did I know the extent of the weeds that would try to take away my garden's water supply. Sadly, I had not marked my plants properly, and I certainly did not make rows of dirt with the roto-tiller. Therefore, I was stuck with waiting until the plants were more mature before attempting to pull out those annoying weeds. Not only did I see the common weeds exploding throughout the beds, but I noticed some very unusual wildflowers that could only have entered through the transplanted soil. I had weeds with huge, prickly protrusions; tall foo-foo-looking stalks branching out in all directions; and other strange plants with round prickly balls. All of those intruders minimized my garden's ability to take in the much needed water.

Likewise, there are some activities that on the surface look like a good thing to do. Certainly, helping someone in need is top on the list. However, doing a good thing can be a bad thing if it takes us away from God's true purpose. When I was young in the Lord, I probably went to church every night of the week. I could not get enough. The fellowship, the study of the Word, and the worship moved me to tears. However, there came a time when my relationship with the Lord needed to be based upon my intimacy with Him rather than on busying myself with the activities at church.

Anything that steals the flow of the Holy Spirit in the believers' life must be pulled out. God longs for intimacy with individuals. His plan is to know us and be known by us (John 10:14). God is faithful to show us our spiritual condition so that we are renewed in our thinking and can adjust our behavior accordingly. Sometimes we are required to let go of that which is "good." Let us look at Abraham and Isaac for instance.

Abraham was promised a son who would carry on the family name and inherit the land that God would show him. Abraham and Sarah "helped God along" by encouraging a surrogate mother. Thus, Hagar produced her offspring, Ishmael. It was not until an angel of the Lord visited the couple and told them they would indeed have a son at such an old age that God followed through with His plans. However, years later, Abraham was required to release Isaac back to God as a test of Abraham's reverence for the Lord (Genesis 22).

Even a good thing can take first place in our hearts. I have had to lay down so many "good" things in my life, but inevitably God replaces the so-called losses with so much better. Recently, we were asked to give up something precious to us. My oldest son has played soccer his whole life. He even aspired to play professionally at some point. However, after playing for three years in college, he was given a choice to either stand for righteousness and lay down soccer, or tolerate ungodly behavior and play.

If it was about him, he may have continued, but he realized that the program and the boys that followed him deserved his righteous stand over his personal comfort. He was required by God to lay down soccer his senior year in college—something we were not ready to give up. However, God had other plans.

In many ways, my son's love of the game of soccer had overshadowed any time he might have spent doing other worthy activities. One of those activities was worshipping God with the drums. Because he had laid down his soccer career his senior year of college, the door opened for him to try out for a group that represented the university. Not only would he be able to pursue his love of worship with the drums, but he would get paid for it. And, would you know, he made the music group and is serving God in a capacity that he could have only dreamt about if he was still playing soccer?

Pruning

I have a violet plant sitting in my kitchen window that was given to me for my birthday eight months ago. For some reason, whenever I receive a plant, it is inevitable that it will die within a short time. Sure enough, after a few weeks, my plant looked dead. At first, I had planned to throw the whole thing away, but something inside me decided to give it another chance. So, I pinched the ugly parts off the plant, watered it and let it be.

A couple months later after faithfully watering a seemingly dead plant, I noticed some new blossoms. I could not believe it. With just a little extra attention given to the plant, it looked new again. And, the Lord did not waste that teachable moment. He began to speak to me about how He was purging me also and that if I would just be patient with what He was doing in me, I would see new growth. Every time I washed my dishes at the window and noticed my violet, I thanked the Lord for the work He was doing in me. And, I also thanked Him for what I was to become after the purging was over.

In the same way, the more I pluck the ripe tomatoes off my plants, the more the blossoms sprout. There were several generations of fruit on those plants that surely could not hold the plant together much longer. Some of the vines began falling to the sides and then, they'd travel across the ground as the fruit bore too heavily on the vine. For quite a long time, I went out to my garden every day to pull more fruit off the vine so that more could be produced. Likewise, we must be pruned periodically so we can grow effectively.

> **I AM** the true vine, and My Father is the husbandman. Every branch in Me that bears not fruit He takes away: and every *branch* that bears fruit, He purges it, that it may bring forth more fruit. Now you are clean through the word which I have spoken to you. Abide in Me, and I in you. As the branch cannot bear fruit of itself, except it abide in the vine; no more can you, except you abide in Me. I am the vine, you are the branches: He that abides in Me, and I in him, the same brings forth much fruit: for without Me you can do nothing. If a man abide not in Me, he is cast forth as a branch, and is withered; and men gather them, and cast them into the fire, and they are burned. If you abide in Me, and My words abide in you, you shall ask what you will, and it shall be done to you. Herein is My Father glorified, that you bear much fruit; so shall you be My disciples.
>
> —John 15:1-8 KJVER

As part of the pruning process, God uses trials in our lives to prune us. I believe He also prunes us by testing us with the Word He has given us. Notice that according to this passage the branches that bear fruit are pruned, first.

In the Parable of the Sower, the person with the stony soil failed to hold the seed because the Word was not able to penetrate the heart during the toughest of trials. We need times of pruning so we can be a doer of the Word. When God gives us a truth, He will usually test us with that same truth. This is where we can see if we really are progressing. And thankfully, if we fail at some point, the Lord will find another way to teach us the same lesson until we get it.

Practical Application

Bible study is not the end of all things. It is not an activity that should fulfill a quota so we can feel better about ourselves. Our relationship with the Lord encompasses so much more than Bible study. However, the Lord (who is the Word) communicates His purposes through the Word to mankind. The Holy Bible is the inspired Word of God, illumined by the Holy Spirit and is made alive in us. The Bible was given for man, out of grace and mercy from God, and it should never become an activity that overrides God's intended work of the Holy Spirit in the believer. The goal of the study of God's Word should be to further God's plan of forming Christ in you, the hope of glory (Colossians 1:27).

Final Thoughts

This chapter on *How We Grow* is an attempt to communicate to you the amazing plan of redemption for mankind, utilizing many elements throughout the growing process. We need the Holy Spirit to teach us all things. In order for the Seed that is within us to burst forth, we must watch what we allow into the soil of our heart and take a regular assessment of our spiritual condition. We must keep out those anointing-stealers and even lay down the good things that can rob us of God's best.

Optimum growth happens when we allow the Holy Spirit to prune us and test us so that we can be doers of the Word.

In the next chapter, *Gardening Tips*, we will transition from the work of the Holy Spirit in the believer and look at how we will study the book of Ruth.

Chapter 4

GARDENING TIPS

THERE ARE SEVERAL ways to study the Bible, but what I will share are some practical tips that will enhance your study. The ideas in this book are certainly not exhaustive, nor are you required to do everything that I suggest. Please allow the Holy Spirit free reign in your heart to do what He wants to do. This is your personal time to study, listen, cry out, and apply the things the Holy Spirit is teaching you. It is a template to be used in the context of the Holy Spirit's directives for you.

I will share the philosophy behind the way we study, the tools I use for study, and then we will actually apply these principles in studying ***Ruth: Road to Redemption*** throughout the remainder of this book.

Philosophy

Due to more than twenty years of home education experience, and the value I have placed on the study of God's Word with my children, I have imparted a great many tools to them. Scripture memory has been a valuable exercise for recall in our household. I prefer to memorize large portions of scripture over individual verses for maximum understanding. It is also helpful to study whole books of the Bible for a panoramic view and an understanding of the context to fully understand the heart of any book of the Bible.

For optimum learning, it is important to read the book (in this case Ruth) through several times and, then, re-tell it in your own words. Right after you read the chapter, there is space created for you to re-tell in your own words what happened. This is not to be mistaken with "Putting It All Together" toward the end of each chapter. This section further allows you to communicate in your own words what the Holy Spirit is saying as it applies to your own life. This is not a time to re-tell the actual story but to relay the spiritual truths gleaned through the story.

If the goal is to retain as much from the Word as possible, then after you read the book through several times, re-tell the story, and answer several questions, this goal should be realized. Some of the answers are obvious and some are not so obvious. You may find yourself going into different books of the Bible to expound on a topic of study. For instance, when you explore the fact that there was a famine in the land and Elimelech took his family to Moab to provide for them, this may inspire you to look into further famines in scripture and how others dealt with famine.

I have broken up your study of the Word into how we should learn any subject. When we study a new language, the first thing we do is learn some of the vocabulary. It also helps to be around those who fluently speak the language for extended periods of time. That is why we read and re-read the book over and over. However, the best way to really learn the language is to live among its speakers and submerge ourselves in the culture full-time. I have been known to stay in certain books in the Bible for months.

- You will **start by doing an individual word study.** I have picked out key words that will bring out a fuller meaning of the text. For instance, some of the names of the people and the places have significant meaning. God does not waste the names. They are there for a reason. So, you will define words from the text itself.

- You will then **look at the literary devices** (an art form used by the author to express ideas through language: i.e. flashback, parable, foreshadowing, irony, oxymoron, personification, poetic justice, symbolism…) used in the narrative.[8] You will not look at the type of literary devices used specifically; however, you will explore those ideas formed through a literary device, mostly to look at the symbolism.

- The initial study up to this point focuses upon the "grammar" or knowledge phase of the material. One last area you will **look at in this stage of study is the historical background of the text.** However, the questions I pose are only a sampling of the thoughts I had while doing the Bible study. You will probably come up with your own word study, symbolism and background notes. Welcome the Holy Spirit's full reign in your heart as you prayerfully study His Word and jot down any questions you may have in the section "Develop Your Own Questions and Answers."

- After the "grammar" of the text is examined, you will move into the "dialogue" or understanding stage. I have provided questions that came to my mind. I bet you did not even realize you are your best communicator as you **dialogue your own thoughts?** Who said there needed to be an audience to do true Bible study? Your audience is the Trinity. Sometimes the Holy Spirit will dialogue with you—posing questions so that He can teach you. Other times, He will point out something that is obvious and you will go on a tangent, only enhancing your study.

- After the dialoguing takes place, it is important to **look at what God is saying about Himself and what He is saying about you** in the chapter. You can usually relate to the characters within the text to some degree. For instance, let us look at Ruth. She is a non-Jew, a pagan living in a foreign land who has decided to embrace Naomi's God. I can relate to her since God literally snatched me out of the kingdom of darkness and placed me in the kingdom of light. I responded to God as she did and because of God's grace, I feel like I am at the threshing floor with Him in preparation for closer intimacy. We can glean from the characters in the story, speaking to us about God and ourselves.

- The final phase of study in *Ruth: Road to Redemption* has to do with **how knowledge and understanding are applied.** It is interesting to note that throughout the Bible we see these same principles used: knowledge, understanding, and wisdom. And really, this is what we are doing when we study the Word this way. We are gaining knowledge through learning the grammar of the subject, dialoguing for further understanding, and finally, applying the knowledge and understanding by using what we know in real life. This is what being a "doer of the Word" really means.

Furthermore, you are given other study opportunities for those of you who would like to master your study. These are mere suggestions, not mandated activities. They do not make you a doer of the Word necessarily, however, learning how to use that which you have studied is something that takes a lifetime to master. But, you will be on the right track if you tackle the knowledge and understanding of the text. Then, it will seem natural to follow through with the testing phase when God challenges you to put the Word into practice in your own life.

The Holy Bible

I have chosen to use the King James Easy-Reading Study Bible[9] simply because it coincides with my Bible study aids. When words are studied in the Hebrew and Greek, the Strong's Concordance matches the words in this version. This is only meant to be used with this Bible study simply for your convenience. I never want to discourage anyone from using their own Bible as a reference.

Bible Aids

Your main tools for study are the *Strong's Exhaustive Concordance* and the *New Unger's Bible Dictionary,* which both can be purchased at any Christian bookstore. The *Strong's Concordance* is used to look up the original Hebrew (or Greek) words in the context of the scripture that is being studied. In the case of Ruth, if you were looking up the word "famine" in the concordance, you would find the word "famine" like you would in a regular dictionary.

Once you find the word, you would look down the list and find the word used in Ruth 1:1. There is an indicator number off to the right side of the word "famine" in Ruth 1:1 (7458). You would then go to the back of the concordance where there are Hebrew listings in the front portion of the indexing and Greek listings in the back of the indexing. Since we are in the Old Testament, you would use the first portion (Hebrew) of the indexing. You would then look up the number (7458) and find the Hebrew definition of "famine."

The Bible Dictionary is used for looking up words much like you would use an encyclopedia. For instance, you could look up the word "Moab" in the Concordance to see what the actual meaning of the word is, but you would also want to look in the Bible dictionary to find out more about Moab, especially when looking into its history. If you would like to utilize both of these on-line tools, here are the web sites:

http://www.studylight.org (Bible Dictionary)
http://www.eliyah.com/lexicon.html (Strong's Concordance)

For the Bible dictionary: type in the given web site in whichever search engine you use on the Internet; on the left-hand side of the page you will see *Study Resources*, click on that button and then Dictionaries. *Holman Bible Dictionary* seems to have the most references available for the student. Click on the first letter of the word for which you are searching. For instance, if you are looking for Moab, click on "M" and then scroll down to Moab/Moabite stone. It will give you the historical background for Moab.

For the *Strong's Concordance* resource: type the given web site into the search engine you use on the Internet. This will take you to the list of concordances available. Click on *Strong's Concordance King James Version* and type in the word you are searching for. For instance, if you are looking up "famine," type in the word "famine" and hit the search button. You will see references from the Bible. Scroll down to Ruth 1:1 and click on 7458. It will give you the lexicon results: the transliteration in Hebrew, pronunciation, root word, part of speech, the biblical usage and definition.

Once you read through the book of Ruth several times, you will be re-telling the first chapter in your own words. You will then be defining terms, using the Bible concordance or dictionary. I have added a feature in our Bible study that will cause you to pause and pray. You will be looking for deeper meaning based upon the literary devices used. You will also look at the historical setting to get fuller understanding of what is going on in the book, and you will answer questions for greater interpretation.

It is my hope that you will develop your own questions at the end of each chapter and then look into those questions as well. You will be looking into who God is in the chapter and who man is as well. You are asked to re-write the chapter based upon the symbolisms you found and draw some spiritual applications from the story. And finally, you are asked to do some additional items called "ideas for mastery" if you want to delve deeper.

I have included my answers in the chapter titled: *Sample Seeds*. However, I must add a **disclaimer**: This Bible study is meant to encourage you, the student, to seek the Lord for His truth. My sample seeds are given so you have an idea of what I am looking for. However, my answers are up for debate. As you pray and seek the Holy Spirit for knowledge and wisdom, and use the true plumb line—God's Word—it is my hope that you will become a Berean.

And the brethren immediately sent away Paul and Si´las by night to Bere´a: who coming *there* went into the synagogue of the Jews. These were more noble than those in Thes-sa-lo-ni´ca, in that they received the word with all readiness of mind, and searched the scriptures daily, whether those things were so.

—Acts 17:10-11 KJVER

Manure, Mulch & Spray

Manure promotes growth. Mulch serves as a protective covering over the soil to modify the effects of the local climate. And spray applications deter unwanted insects. All three of these growth enhancers work alongside Bible study. Let us look at manure first.

When I think of manure, I think of someone else's waste becoming another person's gain. Naomi's family is a great example of this: Elimelech uprooted his family from Bethlehem-Judah—"The House of Bread" and moved them to a place of physical abundance, but spiritual decadence. Elimelech sacrificed his spiritual food for physical food. Instead of staying in Moab temporarily, he must have established a business, a nice livelihood, and comfort for himself and his family, indefinitely.

This was a detrimental decision on Elimelech's part because he ended up losing his life prematurely and eventually losing his boys' hearts to the Moabite culture. They also died prematurely, thus, leaving three ladies without a name, inheritance, or any children.

It is important that we study the Bible with an intuitiveness that causes us to look at the 'dung' in other's lives so we do not repeat their mistakes. I wonder why Elimelech was willing to lay down his culture, people, land, and even possibly his God for his economic and physical comfort? And how did this affect Naomi? What was her spiritual condition in the aftermath of the deaths of her husband and two sons? I do not want to give away the whole story, however, for the purpose of application, it is important that you read the text with an eye for what can be learned from the characters' waste.

Likewise, when I think of mulch, I think of usefulness because it is really recycled waste. Something that was used for enjoyment: take a tree with large climbing branches for example, that suddenly gets blown over by hurricane force winds and is cut down, cut into pieces, and made into chipped wood for another person's use. The material changes from one function to another while maintaining the same property. However, mulch is used to protect the soil from the hot sun, leaving the rainwater intact for a longer period of time.

This brings me to how we keep the anointing of the Holy Spirit upon us for longer periods of time. We are warned against quenching the Spirit (1 Thessalonians 5:19). The word *quench* in the Greek means to not extinguish[10] the Holy Spirit.

You may be wondering how you would extinguish the Holy Spirit. This happens when the Word is only studied but not applied. There is something the Holy Spirit wants each of us to learn from our study and He certainly wants us to retain what we learn so we can later apply it.

Furthermore, spray applications are sometimes necessary to prevent a premature harvest because of pesky insects. We must guard the Word of God implanted within our hearts. The Holy Spirit not only teaches us all things but we will have a test when we are done. The test is to see if the Word has truly taken root in our hearts. The only way to keep the Word alive is to work it out in each of our lives.

> For every one that uses milk is unskillful in the word of righteousness: for he is a babe. But strong meat belongs to them that are of full age, *even* those who by reason of use have their senses exercised to discern both good and evil.
>
> —Hebrews 5:13-14 KJVER

We can actually train ourselves in the Word as we exercise our spiritual muscles and apply the Word of God to our lives in every situation. So, with this in mind, I encourage you to read the Word and study **Ruth: Road to Redemption** with a commitment for a spiritual workout.

One Final Gardening Tip

We can look at the analogy of hybrid versus non-hybrid seeds by looking at the seeds we are collecting. Are we collecting seeds from the original source or are we cross-pollinating? I prefer to study the scriptures using the original source as much as possible. This means going to the original Greek and Hebrew words rather than looking at a commentary. This also means relying upon the Holy Spirit to teach me the Word and its proper application rather than taking someone else's regurgitated food. And finally, this means keeping my main-stay the personal study of God's Word rather than for the purpose of upholding the doctrines of men.

It is so easy to begin our study using the lens of the traditions of men rather than spending the time to search the scriptures for ourselves. In order for us to be fruitful, we must do a thorough study of God's Word from His original intent, rather from the basis of men's doctrines. We want the pure seed, not a cross-pollinated one that loses its full potential from one generation to the next. So, let us begin studying ***Ruth: Road to Redemption*** with simply God's seed—His Word.

Chapter 5

AWAY FROM THE HOUSE OF BREAD — RUTH, CHAPTER I

Bible Study Checklist

- ☐ Read through the whole book of Ruth several times using your own Bible.

- ☐ Retrieve your Bible study aids—*Strong's Concordance* and *Bible Dictionary.*

- ☐ Read Ruth, Chapter 1 as provided.

- ☐ Re-write the chapter in the space provided (see Appendix I for an example).

- ☐ Define the words in the *Strong's Concordance* or in the *Bible Dictionary.* (See possible answers in Sample Seeds in Chapter Ten.)

- ☐ Answer the questions for symbolism under literary devices. (See possible answers in *Sample Seeds* in Chapter Ten.)

☐   Explore the historical applications. (See possible answers in *Sample Seeds* in Chapter Ten.)

☐   Look at God and man's character in the context of Ruth 1. (See possible answers in *Sample Seeds* in Chapter Ten.)

☐   Re-write Ruth, chapter 1 with the applied symbolism in mind. (See Appendix II for an example.)

☐   Do the mastery ideas if you are ambitious. (See possible answers in *Sample Seeds* in Chapter Ten.)

☐   Write out your own questions and find the answers.

Ruth 1

¹**NOW** it came to pass in the days when the judges ruled, that there was a famine in the land. And a certain man of Beth´-le-hem-ju´dah went to sojourn in the country of Mo´ab, he, and his wife, and his two sons. ²And the name of the man *was* E-lim´e-lech, and the name of his wife Na-o´mi, and the name of his two sons Mah´lon and Chil´i-on, Eph´rath-ites of Beth´-le-hem-judah. And they came into the country of Mo´ab, and continued there. ³And E-lim´e-lech Na-o´mi's husband died; and she was left, and her two sons. ⁴And they took them wives of the women of Mo´ab; the name of the one *was* Or´pah, and the name of the other Ruth: and they dwelled there about ten years. ⁵And Mah´lon and Chil´i-on died also both of them; and the woman was left of her two sons and her husband. ⁶Then she arose with her daughters in law, that she might return from the country of Mo´ab: for she had

heard in the country of Mo´ab how that the LORD had visited His people in giving them bread. ⁷Wherefore she went forth out of the place where she was, and her two daughters in law with her; and they went on the way to return to the land of Ju´dah. ⁸And Na-o´mi said to her two daughters in law, Go, return each to her mother's house: the LORD deal kindly with you, as you have dealt with the dead, and with me. ⁹The LORD grant that you may find rest, each of you in the house of her husband. Then she kissed them; and they lifted up their voice, and wept. ¹⁰And they said to her, Surely we will return with you to your people. ¹¹And Na-o´mi said, Turn again, my daughters: why will you go with me? *are* there yet any more sons in my womb, that they may be your husbands? ¹²Turn again, my daughters, go your way; for I am too old to have a husband. *If* I should say, I have hope, if I should have a husband also to night, and should also bear sons; ¹³Would you tarry for them till they were grown? would you stay for them from having husbands? nay, my daughters; for it grieves me much for your sakes that the hand of the LORD is gone out against me. ¹⁴And they lifted up their voice, and wept again: and Or´pah kissed her mother in law; but Ruth clung to her. ¹⁵And she said, Behold, your sister in law is gone back to her people, and to her gods: return you after your sister in law. ¹⁶And Ruth said, Entreat me not to leave you, *or* to return from following after you: for where you go, I will go; and where you lodge, I will lodge: your people *shall be* my people, and your God my God: ¹⁷Where you die, will I die, and there will I be buried: the LORD do so to me, and more also, *if anything* but death part you and me. ¹⁸When she saw that she was steadfastly minded to go with her, then she left speaking to her. [19]So they two went until they came to Beth´-le-hem. And it came to pass, when they were come to Beth´-le-hem, that all the city was moved about them, and they said, *Is* this Na-o´mi? [20]And she said to them, Call me not Na-o´mi, call me Ma ´ra: for the Almighty has dealt very bitterly with me. [21]I went out full, and the LORD has brought me home again empty: why *then* call you me Na-o´mi, seeing the LORD has testified against me, and the Almighty has afflicted me? [22]So Na-o´mi returned, and Ruth the Mo´ab-it-ess, her daughter in law, with her, which returned out of the country of Mo´ab: and they came to Beth´-le-hem in the beginning of barley harvest. (KJVER)

A. **Rewrite Ruth, Chapter One and give it a title.** (See example in Appendix I.)

B. Define the following names/words, using the Strong's Concordance or the Bible dictionary. Look the word up in the context of the passage and find the indicator number in the back of the Strong's Concordance under the Hebrew index. Your personal Bible may have some of the meanings in its Concordance as well. Record new meanings in the Bible text provided. (Sample answers can be found in *Sample Seeds* in Chapter Ten).

Famine

Moab

Bethlehem-Judah

Elimelech

Naomi

Mahlon

Chilion

Orpah

Ruth

Mara

C. Answer the following questions using the text provided. (Sample answers can be found in *Sample Seeds* in Chapter Ten).

1. What is Naomi saying when she tells the women to call her Mara instead of Naomi?

2. How many times did Naomi tell her daughters-in-law to return to their land of origin? Is there any significance to that number?

D. **Historical background.** (Sample answers can be found in *Sample Seeds* in Chapter Ten.)

1. Find out more about Moab in the Bible Dictionary.

2. The days when the judges ruled are the background of this story. What was going on during this time? Look in the back of your personal Bible under judges for scripture references or find out when this time period was and read what the Bible Dictionary says.

3. Who was Elimelech (Tribe of Judah)? Why did he leave his homeland to go to Moab? What was going on during this time?

E. **Questions for personal application.** (Sample answers can be found in *Sample Seeds* in Chapter Ten.)

1. Was it Elimelech's plan to stay in Moab indefinitely? Look up the word *sojourn* (verse 1).

2. What kept Naomi in Moab originally?

3. What was the reason for Orpah's decision to stay and Ruth's decision to go?

4. Why did Naomi want to return to her homeland and what were the reasons she used to persuade her daughters-in-law to return to their families?

5. What was the blessing Naomi spoke over her daughters-in-law (vs. 8-9)?

6. Compare Orpah and Ruth. What was their commitment level?

7. What was Ruth's commitment to Naomi?

8. When did they return? In what season? What is the significance of barley?

9. Did the women recognize Naomi? Why or why not?

10. What did Naomi believe about God?

F. **God's Character Revealed.** (Sample answers can be found in *Sample Seeds* in Chapter Ten).

1. What can we learn about God in this chapter?

G. **Man's Character Revealed in this chapter.** (Sample answers can be found in *Sample Seeds* in Chapter Ten.)

1. What would you do if there was a famine in your land?

2. Is it okay to be unequally yoked in marriage? Find scripture to back up your response.

H. Putting It All Together:

Re-write Chapter One in your own words, using the symbolism found, and pray for revelation from the Holy Spirit. (See Appendix II for an example.)

I. **Ideas for Mastery.** (Sample answers can be found in *Sample Seeds* in Chapter Ten).

1. According to Jewish law, was it okay to marry foreign women?

2. Look up scriptures that talk about the one new man—Jew and Gentile. See Ephesians 2:15-3:7. Also, look at scriptures about how the Gentiles were grafted in (Romans 11:1-25). What does this have to do with Naomi and Ruth?

J. **Develop Your Own Questions and Answers**

Chapter 6

THE BEGINNING OF HARVEST – RUTH, CHAPTER 2

Bible Study Checklist

☐ Read Ruth, Chapter 2 as provided.

☐ Re-write the chapter in the space provided. (See Appendix I for an example.)

☐ Define the words in the Strong's Concordance or in the Bible Dictionary. (See possible answers in *Sample Seeds* in Chapter Ten.)

☐ Answer the questions for symbolism under literary devices. (See possible answers in *Sample Seeds* in Chapter Ten.)

☐ Explore the historical applications. (See possible answers in *Sample Seeds* in Chapter Ten.)

☐ Look at God and man's character in the context of Ruth 2. (See possible answers in *Sample Seeds* in Chapter Ten.)

☐   Re-write Ruth, chapter 2 in your own words, using the symbolism found. (See Appendix II for an example.)

☐   Do the mastery ideas if you are ambitious. (See possible answers in *Sample Seeds* in Chapter Ten.)

☐   Write out your own questions and find the answers.

Ruth 2

[1]**AND** Na-o'mi had a kinsman of her husband's, a mighty man of wealth, of the family of E-lim'e-lech; and his name *was* Bo'az. [2]And Ruth the Mo'ab-it-ess said to Na-o'mi, Let me now go to the field, and glean ears of corn after *him* in whose sight I shall find grace. And she said to her, Go, my daughter. [3]And she went, and came, and gleaned in the field after the reapers: and her hap was to light on a part of the field *belonging* to Bo'az, *who* was of the kindred of E-lim'e-lech. [4]And behold, Bo'az came from Beth'-le-hem, and said to the reapers, The LORD *be* with you. And they answered him, The LORD bless you. [5]Then said Bo'az to his servant that was set over the reapers, Whose damsel *is* this? [6]And the servant that was set over the reapers answered and said, It *is* the Mo'ab-it-ish damsel that came back with Na-o'mi out of the country of Mo'ab: [7]And she said, I pray you, let me glean and gather after the reapers among the sheaves: so she came, and has continued even from the morning until now, that she tarried a little in the house. [8]Then said Bo'az to Ruth, Hear you not, my daughter? Go not to glean in another field, neither go from here, but abide here fast by my maidens: [9]*Let* your eyes *be* on the field that they do reap,

and go you after them: have I not charged the young men that they shall not touch you? and when you are thirsty, go to the vessels, and drink of *that* which the young men have drawn. [10]Then she fell on her face, and bowed herself to the ground, and said to him, Why have I found grace in your eyes, that you should take knowledge of me, seeing I *am* a stranger? [11]And Bo´az answered and said to her, It has fully been showed me, all that you have done to your mother in law since the death of your husband: and *how* you have left your father and your mother, and the land of your nativity, and are come to a people which you knew not before. [12]The Lord recompense your work, and a full reward be given you of the Lord God of Is´ra-el, under whose wings you are come to trust. [13]Then she said, Let me find favor in your sight, my lord; for that you have comforted me, and for that you have spoken friendly to your handmaid, though I be not like to one of your handmaidens. [14]And Bo´az said to her, At mealtime come you here, and eat of the bread, and dip your morsel in the vinegar. And she sat beside the reapers: and he reached her parched *corn*; and she did eat, and was sufficed, and left. [15]And when she was risen up to glean, Bo´az commanded his young men, saying, Let her glean even among the sheaves, and reproach her not; [16]And let fall also some of the handfuls of purpose for her, and leave them, that she may glean them, and rebuke her not. [17]So she gleaned in the field until evening, and beat out that she had gleaned: and it was about an ephah of barley. [18]And she took *it* up, and went into the city: and her mother in law saw what she had gleaned: and she brought forth, and gave to her that she had reserved after she was sufficed. [19]And her mother in law said to her, Where have you gleaned to day? Where worked you? blessed be he that did take knowledge of you. And she showed her mother in law with whom she had worked, and said, The man's name with whom I worked to day *is* Bo´az. [20]And Na-o´mi said to her daughter in law, Blessed *be* he of the LORD, who has not left off His kindness to the living and to the dead. And Na-o´mi said to her, The man *is* near of kin to us, one of our next kinsman. [21]And Ruth the Mo´ab-it-ess said, he said to me also, you shall keep fast by my young men, until they have ended all my harvest. [22]And Na-o´mi said to Ruth her daughter in law, *It is* good, my daughter, that you go out with his maidens, that they meet you not in any other field. [23]So she kept fast by the maidens of Bo´az to glean to the end of barley harvest and of wheat harvest; and dwelled with her mother in law. (KJVER)

A. Re-write Ruth, Chapter Two and give it a Summation Title. (See example in Appendix I.)

B. Themes and Symbolism from the text and their meanings.

Note: Record new meanings in the Bible text provided. Sample answers can be found in *Sample Seeds* in Chapter Ten. (Remember: Look the word up in the context of the passage and find the indicator number in the back of the *Strong's Concordance* under the Hebrew index. Your personal Bible may have some of the meanings in the back of your Bible in the concordance as well.)

Kinsman

Grace

Sheaves

Stranger

Trust

Favor

Lord

Purpose

Sufficed

Maidens

C. Literary Devices. (Sample answers can be found in Sample Seeds in Chapter Ten.)

1. In verses 8 and 21 there is a possible contradiction. The narration states that Boaz told Ruth not to glean in another field (verse 8) but abide close to his maidens. She then tells Naomi (verse 21) that she was told by Boaz to stay close by his young men until the end of the harvest. And in verse 22, Naomi admonishes her to keep close to the maidens. Did she misunderstand? Why the discrepancy?

2. What does the phrase "under whose wings you have come to trust" mean?

3. What is the spiritual significance of Ruth eating the bread and dipping it in vinegar at Boaz's table?

D. **Historical Setting.** (Sample answers can be found in *Sample Seeds* in Chapter Ten.)

1. Read scripture on the kinsman redeemer. Find out his purpose and the rules governing him?

2. What is the background behind reaping and gathering in another's field? Who is allowed to do this and why? Can a person gather after the reapers among the sheaves normally? What is a handful of purpose?

E. **Questions for personal application.** (Sample answers can be found in *Sample Seeds* in Chapter Ten.)

1. Was Ruth's experience in Boaz's field on purpose or a coincidence? (See verse 3.)

2. Did Boaz know Ruth?

3. What did Boaz instruct Ruth to do?

4. What did Boaz learn of Ruth through his servants?

5. What is the difference between grace and favor?

6. What did Boaz instruct his young men to do?

7. How much is an ephah of barley? What is a handful of purpose?

8. What did Naomi discover and what was her reaction?

9. What did Naomi instruct Ruth to do?

F. **God's Character Revealed.** (Sample answers can be found in *Sample Seeds* in Chapter Ten.)

1. Who is God in this chapter?

G. Our Character Revealed. (Sample answers can be found in *Sample Seeds* in Chapter Ten.)

1. What is required of man according to this chapter?

2. Naomi seems to see God's hand for the first time in a long time. Who does God use to turn Naomi's heart around? What is the spiritual significance?

H. Putting it all together.

Re-write Chapter Two in your own words, using the spiritual symbolism found, and pray for revelation from the Holy Spirit. (See sample in Appendix II.)

I. **Ideas for Mastery.** (Sample answers can be found in *Sample Seeds* in Chapter Ten.)

1. Research the origins of communion and its spiritual significance.

2. Look at the laws of the kinsman redeemer and how Jesus fulfilled them for us.

J. Write out your own questions and find the answers.

Chapter 7

AT THE THRESHING FLOOR – RUTH, CHAPTER 3

Bible Study Checklist

☐ Read Ruth, Chapter 3 as provided.

☐ Re-write the chapter in the space provided. (See Appendix I for an example.)

☐ Define the words in the *Strong's Concordance* or in the *Bible Dictionary*. (See possible answers in *Sample Seeds* in Chapter Ten.)

☐ Answer the questions for symbolism under literary devices. (See possible answers in *Sample Seeds* in Chapter Ten.)

☐ Explore the historical applications. (See possible answers in *Sample Seeds* in Chapter Ten.)

☐ Look at God and man's character in the context of Ruth 3. (See possible answers in *Sample Seeds* in Chapter Ten.)

☐ Re-write Ruth, Chapter 3 in your own words, using the spiritual applications you find. (See Appendix II for an example.)

☐ Do the mastery ideas if you are ambitious. (See possible answers in *Sample Seeds* in Chapter Ten.)

☐ Write out your own questions and find the answers.

Ruth 3

[1]**THEN** Na-o'mi her mother in law said to her, My daughter, shall I not seek rest for you, that it may be well with you? [2]And now *is* not Bo'az of our kindred, with whose maidens you were? Behold, he winnows barley tonight in the threshingfloor. [3]Wash yourself therefore, and anoint you, put your raiment upon you, and get you down to the floor: *but* make not yourself known to the man, until he shall have done eating and drinking. [4]And it shall be, when he lies down, that you shall mark the place where he shall lie; and you shall go in, and uncover his feet, and lay you down; and he will tell you what you shall do. [5]And she said to her, All that you say to me I will do. [6]And she went down to the floor, and did according to all that her mother in law bid her. [7]And when Bo'az had eaten and drunk, and his heart was merry, he went to lie down at the end of the heap of corn: and she came softly, and uncovered his feet, and laid her down. [8]And it came to pass at midnight, that the man was afraid, and turned himself: and, behold, a woman lay at his feet. [9]And he said, Who *are* you? And she answered, I *am* Ruth your handmaid: spread therefore your skirt over your handmaid; for you *are* a near kinsman. [10]And he

said, Blessed *be* you of the LORD, my daughter: for you have showed more kindness in the latter end than at the beginning, inasmuch as you followed not young men, whether poor or rich. ¹¹And now, my daughter, fear not; I will do to you all that you require: for all the city of my people does know that you *are* a virtuous woman. ¹²And now it is true that I *am your* near kinsman: however there is a kinsman nearer than I. ¹³Tarry this night, and it shall be in the morning, *that* if he will perform to you the part of a kinsman, well; let him do the kinsman's part: but if he will not do the part of a kinsman to you, then will I do the part of a kinsman to you, *as* the LORD lives: lie down until the morning.

¹⁴And she lay at his feet until the morning: and she rose up before one could know another. And he said, Let it not be known that a woman came into the floor. ¹⁵Also he said, Bring the veil that *you have* upon you, and hold it. And when she held it, he measured six *measures* of barley, and laid *it* on her: and she went into the city. ¹⁶And when she came to her mother in law, she said, Who are you, my daughter? And she told her all that the man had done to her. ¹⁷And she said, These six *measures* of barley gave he me; for he said to me, Go not empty to your mother in law. ¹⁸Then said she, Sit still, my daughter, until you know how the matter will fall: for the man will not be in rest, until he have finished the thing this day. (KJVER)

A. Rewrite Ruth, Chapter 3 and give it a Summation Title. (See Appendix I for an example.)

B. Themes and Symbolism from the text and their meanings.

Note: Record new meanings in the Bible text provided. Sample answers can be found in *Sample Seeds* in Chapter Ten. (Remember: Look the word up in the context of the passage and find the indicator number in the back of the *Strong's Concordance* under the Hebrew index. Your personal Bible may have some of the meanings in the back of your Bible in the Concordance as well).

Rest

Wash

Anoint

Mark

Virtuous

C. **Literary Devices.** (Sample answers can be found in Sample Seeds in Chapter Ten.)

1. What was Naomi seeking for Ruth?

2. What was required of Ruth before she went to the threshing floor? What is the spiritual significance?

3. There is quite a bit of symbolism in this chapter. What do you think the near kinsman and the nearer kinsman represent? Why six measures of barley?

4. What was Naomi asking Ruth in verse 16?

5. Why do you think Naomi was so sure of Boaz's responsibility being fulfilled that day?

D. Historical Setting. (Sample answers can be found in *Sample Seeds* in Chapter Ten.)

1. Look at the significance of uncovering the feet, lying down and asking for his skirt to cover her? Why at the threshing floor?

2. Why must he go to the nearer kinsman first?

E. Questions for Personal Application. (Sample answers can be found in *Sample Seeds* in Chapter Ten.)

1. What was Ruth's response to Naomi after being instructed as to what she should do? See verses 5-6.

2. Why was Boaz lying at the pile of grain?

3. Look at Boaz's response to Ruth's nearness. What was he saying to her?

4. Why did she arise early?

F. **God's Character Revealed.** (Sample answers can be found in *Sample Seeds* in Chapter Ten.)

1. If Boaz is a type of Christ, what is God saying in this chapter?

2. What is God's part in redemption?

G. **Our Character Revealed.** (Sample answers can be found in *Sample Seeds* in Chapter Ten.)

1. If Naomi represents the Jews and Ruth represents the Gentiles, what is this chapter saying about man?

2. What is required of man to be redeemed?

H. Putting it all together.

Re-write Ruth, Chapter Three in your own words, using the symbolism found, and pray for revelation from the Holy Spirit. (See example in Appendix II.)

I. Ideas for Mastery:

1. Research the process of harvesting grain. How does this relate to you spiritually?

2. Find out what six measures of barley represent. What does the number six symbolize based on other scriptures?

J. Write out your own questions and find the answers.

Chapter 8

FRUITFULNESS — RUTH, CHAPTER 4

Bible Study Checklist

☐ Read Ruth, Chapter 4 as provided.

☐ Re-write the chapter in the space provided (see Appendix I for an example)

☐ Define the words in the *Strong's Concordance* or in the Bible dictionary. (See possible answers in *Sample Seeds* in Chapter Ten.)

☐ Answer the questions for symbolism under literary devices. (See possible answers in *Sample Seeds* in Chapter Ten.)

☐ Explore the historical applications. (See possible answers in *Sample Seeds* in Chapter Ten.)

☐ Look at God and man's character in the context of Ruth 4. (See possible answers in *Sample Seeds* in Chapter Ten.)

☐   Re-write Ruth, chapter 4 in your own words, using the symbolism found. (See Appendix II for an example.)

☐   Do the mastery ideas if you are ambitious. (See possible answers in *Sample Seeds* in Chapter Ten.)

☐   Write out your own questions and find the answers

Ruth 4

[1]**THEN** went Bo′az up to the gate, and sat him down there: and, behold, the kinsman of whom Bo′az spoke came by; to whom he said, Ho, such a one! turn aside, and sit down here. And he turned aside, and sat down. [2]And he took ten men of the elders of the city, and said, Sit you down here. And they sat down. [3]And he said to the kinsman, Na-o′mi, that is come again out of the country of Mo′ab, sells a parcel of land, which was our brother E-lim′e-lech's: [4]And I thought to advertise you, saying, Buy *it* before the inhabitants, and before the elders of my people. If you will redeem *it*, redeem it: but if you will not redeem *it, then* tell me, that I may know: for *there is* none to redeem *it* beside you; and I *am* after you. And he said, I will redeem *it*. [5]Then said Bo′az, What day you buy the field of the hand of Na-o′mi, you must buy *it* also of Ruth the Mo′ab-it-ess, the wife of the dead, to raise up the name of the dead upon his inheritance. [6]And the kinsman said, I cannot redeem *it* for myself, lest I mar my own inheritance: redeem you my right to yourself; for I cannot redeem *it*. [7]Now this *was the manner* in former time in Is′ra-el concerning redeeming and concerning changing, for to confirm all things; a

man plucked off his shoe, and gave *it* to his neighbor: and this *was* a testimony in Is'ra-el. [8]Therefore the kinsman said to Bo'az, Buy *it* for you. So he drew off his shoe. [9]And Bo'az said to the elders, and to all the people, You *are* witnesses this day, that I have bought all that was E-lim'e-lech's, and all that *was* Chil'i-on's and Mah'lon's, of the hand of Na-o'mi. [10]Moreover Ruth the Mo'ab-it-ess, the wife of Mah'lon, have I purchased to be my wife, to raise up the name of the dead upon his inheritance, that the name of the dead be not cut off from among his brethren, and from the gate of his place: you *are* witnesses this day. [11]And all the people that *were* in the gate, and the elders, said, *We are* witnesses. The LORD make the woman that is come into your house like Ra'chel and like Le'ah, which two did build the house of Is'ra-el: and do you worthily in Eph'ra-tah, and be famous in Beth'le-hem: [12]And let your house be like the house of Pha 'rez, whom Ta'mar bore to Ju'dah, of the seed which the LORD shall give you of this young woman. [13]So Bo'az took Ruth, and she was his wife: and when he went in to her, the LORD gave her conception, and she bore a son. [14]And the women said to Na-o'mi, Blessed *be* the LORD, which has not left you this day without a kinsman, that his name may be famous in Is'ra-el. [15]And he shall be to you a restorer of *your* life, and a nourisher of your old age: for your daughter in law, which loves you, which is better to you than seven sons, has born him. [16]And Na-o'mi took the child, and laid it in her bosom, and became nurse to it. [17]And the women her neighbors gave it a name, saying, There is a son born to Na-o'mi; and they called his name O'bed: he *is* the father of Jes'se, the father of Da'vid. [18]Now these *are* the generations of Pha'rez: Pha'rez fathered Hez'ron, [19]And Hez'ron fathered Ram, and Ram fathered Am-min'a-dab, [20]And Am-min'a-dab fathered Nah'shon, and Nah'shon fathered Sal'mon, [21]And Sal'mon fathered Bo'az, and Bo'az fathered O'bed, [22]And O'bed fathered Jes'se, and Jes'se fathered Da'vid.

A. Re-write Ruth, Chapter Four and Give it a Summation Title. (See Appendix I for an example.)

B. Themes and Symbolism from the text and their meanings.

Note: Record new meanings in the Bible text provided. Sample answers can be found in *Sample Seeds* in Chapter Ten. Look the word up in the context of the passage and find the indicator number in the back of the *Strong's Concordance* under the Hebrew index. Your personal Bible may have some of the meanings in the back of your Bible in the Concordance as well.

Gate

Redeem

Mar

Witnesses

Purchased

Restorer

Nourisher

Obed

C. **Literary Devices.** (Sample answers can be found in *Sample Seeds* in Chapter Ten.)

1. Why did Boaz tell the nearer kinsman only about the parcel of land and not about Ruth at the front end of his conversation?

2. There was a blessing spoken by the witnesses over Boaz in verses 11-12. What were they saying?

3. The women said to Naomi, "for your daughter-in-law who loves you is better to you than seven sons, has born him." What do the seven sons represent?

D. Historical Setting. (Sample answers can be found in *Sample Seeds* in Chapter Ten.)

1. Look into how a person confirms all things in scriptures (verses 7-8).

2. Read about Rachel and Leah so you can compare what the blessing over Ruth really means.

3. Read about the house of Pharez and figure out what Boaz's blessing meant.

4. Why are the generations listed?

E. Questions and Answers for Personal Application. (Sample answers can be found in *Sample Seeds* in Chapter Ten.)

1. Why were ten men of the elders of the city asked to join Boaz?

2. Why was Ruth included in the kinsman redeemer deal?

3. Why did the nearer kinsman refuse to redeem Ruth?

4. Why did Naomi take the child, lay him in her bosom and become his nurse rather than Ruth?

5. Why did the women neighbors name the boy, Obed? What did they proclaim?

6. How many generations are mentioned in verses 18-22?

7. Who was worthy in Ephratah and famous in Bethlehem according to the Gospels?

F. **God's Character Revealed.** (Sample answers can be found in *Sample Seeds* in Chapter Ten.)

1. If Boaz is a type of Christ, what did you learn about Him?

2. If the nearer kinsman is the type of the law, what did you learn?

G. Our Character Revealed. (Sample answers can be found in *Sample Seeds* in Chapter Ten.)

1. If Naomi represents the Jews, and Ruth represents the Gentiles who are grafted in, what can you learn about both?

H. Putting It All Together:

1. Re-write Ruth, Chapter Four in your own words using the symbolism found and pray for revelation from the Holy Spirit. (See example in Appendix II.)

I. Ideas for Mastery. (Sample answers can be found in *Sample Seeds* in Chapter Ten.)

1. Research the Levirate law.

2. Find scripture that talks about ten generations and what can happen when that time expires.

J. Develop your own questions and find the answers.

Chapter 9

GLEANING FROM THE BOOK OF RUTH

THERE ARE SO many themes and sub-themes in the book of Ruth. Even though I have studied the four chapters of Ruth for a combined total of nine months, and you have just spent time studying this Bible study within the template I have created for you, there is so much more to experience. If we are to know, understand, and apply what we have learned, now is a good time to review some of the lessons learned from **Ruth: Road to Redemption**. We cannot allow ourselves to be cut short from what the Lord wants to do in our lives through that which we have gleaned. It is my prayer that the truths of Ruth will go down into the depths of your heart so that your life will bear much fruit.

Famine in the Land

When there is a lack of food, physically or spiritually, we must examine why. According to Deuteronomy 28, there are blessings and curses based upon those who hearken diligently to the voice of the Lord and observe to do all the commandments of the Lord.

And the LORD shall make you plenteous in goods, in the fruit of your body, and in the fruit of your cattle, and in the fruit of your ground, in the land which the LORD swore to your fathers to give you.

—Deuteronomy 28:11 KJVER

Cursed *shall you be* in the city, and cursed *shall you be* in the field. Cursed *shall be* your basket and your store. Cursed *shall be* the fruit of your body, and the fruit of your land, the increase of your cattle and the flocks of your sheep.

—Deuteronomy 28:16-18 KJVER

The first thing we should do is ask ourselves when there is great lack: Am I hearkening diligently to the voice of the Lord and doing His commandments?

Furthermore, if famine is not the direct result of personal disobedience, it may be the direct result of sin in those around you. Nevertheless, it is a time to seek God's guidance on what to do about the famine. This is not the time to figure things out according to human reasoning either. Elimelech made a decision to uproot his family and live in an ungodly, foreign land instead of deal with the famine in his land. However, when famine struck Joseph in the land of Egypt, the Lord spoke to him in a dream. Because he was a man who listened to the Lord, God gave him strategies for saving the seed during the seven years of plenty, so that he could have enough during the seven years of drought (Genesis 41).

Both men made a choice. One man fought by preparing and the other took flight. Whatever the reason for the famine, God is looking for men/women who will rely upon the Spirit of God during a period of much lack, rather than trust in human reasoning.

Identity Crisis

We have all gone through tough times in our lives, some more than others. I can relate to Naomi in many ways. I have not lost a husband or a child, but I have lost a brother to murder and a sister due to an ungodly lifestyle. Both prematurely. I can understand why Naomi felt she was being judged by God, but she obviously did not have a proper view of Him. She lived in a decadent culture that had an abundance of physical food and comforts, but lacked in the area of spiritual food. Maybe, Naomi was a victim of her husband's decision to go to the land of "plenty" over the land where God dwelt; however, God gave her another chance to get things right.

I love the way the Lord showed Himself to Naomi throughout her seemingly bleak future. God restored her understanding of who He is—merciful, gracious, involved in the affairs of mankind, a provider, caregiver of the family name, inheritance, and the future generations. Everything a mother cares about. Naomi became a surrogate mother to Ruth, teaching her the laws and customs of the Jewish people—the provisional law that allowed the poor to glean in someone else's field, the Levirate Law that gave a family member permission to marry a deceased man's wife, and the protocol necessary to entreat a kinsman redeemer. Naomi knew all these things and imparted them to Ruth. Throughout Naomi's crisis of identity—knowing who God is and what her purpose was, God lovingly showed her both.

The Cost of Discipleship

Ruth had no idea what her life would look like when she made the commitment to follow Naomi's God. As far as she was concerned, her physical comforts were over. She left her land, people, family, and gods to embrace the God of Abraham, Isaac, and Jacob. Her decision was not taken lightly because Naomi certainly poured on the debate tactics, trying to convince her she had no future in Bethlehem-Judah—"The House of Bread." Ruth had to tell Naomi no, four times. Even her sister-in-law, Orpah, finally gave in to Naomi's reasoning. Regardless of Naomi's logic, Ruth stood by her commitment.

What did Ruth have to gain by moving to a foreign country? She would be an outcast, dependent upon others for her provision. Certainly not someone with status, power, or prestige. She would possibly be subjected to hard labor, busybodies, and patronizing workers. So, why did she submit to Naomi and Boaz's counsel? What did she have to gain?

We can ask the same thing of Jesus' disciples. Why did they drop everything: their careers, home life, and family to follow Jesus? The cost of discipleship is everything.

> So likewise, whosoever he be of you that forsakes not all that he has, he cannot be My disciple.
>
> —Luke 14:33 KJVER

> Then said Je'sus to His disciples, If any *man* will come after Me, let him deny himself, and take up his cross, and follow Me. For whosoever will save his life shall lose it: and whosoever will lose his life for My sake shall find it. For what is a man profited, if he shall gain the whole world, and lose his own soul? or what shall a man give in exchange for his soul?
>
> —Matthew 16:24-26 KJVER

Let's look at the rich young ruler in the Gospel of Luke.

> And a certain ruler asked Him, saying, Good Master, what shall I do to inherit eternal life? And Je'sus said to him, Why call you Me good? none is good, save One, that is, God. You know the commandments, Do not commit adultery, Do not kill, Do not steal, Do not bear false witness, Honor your father and your mother. And he said, All these have I kept from my youth up. Now when Je'sus heard these things, He said to him, Yet lack you one thing: sell all that you have, and distribute to the poor, and you shall have treasure in heaven: and come, follow Me. And when he heard this, he was very sorrowful: for he was very rich. And when Je'sus saw that he was very sorrowful, He said, How hardly shall they that have riches enter into the kingdom of God! For it is easier for a camel to go through a needle's eye, than for a rich man to enter into the kingdom of God. And they that heard it said, Who

then can be saved? And He said, The things which are impossible with men are possible with God. Then Pe´ter said, Lo, we have left all, and followed You. And He said to them, Verily I say to you, There is no man that has left house, or parents, or brethren, or wife, or children, for the kingdom of God's sake, Who shall not receive manifold more in this present time, and in the world to come life everlasting.

—Luke 18:18-30 KJVER

The point of this dialogue is not the fact that the man was rich. It was because something in his life—his riches—was too important to him. In order to be a true disciple of Christ, he had to let go of whatever took first place in his heart. In the same way, God wants first place in our hearts. God is no respecter of persons (Romans 2:11). If He requires Ruth, the disciples and the rich young ruler to leave behind all, this is the same standard we must embrace. The cost of following Jesus is everything.

Submission/Obedience/Authority

Ruth revered Naomi, Boaz, and Naomi's God. Naomi was Ruth's mother-in-law and mentor. Boaz was her overseer and provider. And Naomi's God was someone she was getting to know. Ruth's attitude was one of humility (dependence upon someone other than herself) for survival. She lived in a foreign country with strange customs and laws, which she could follow through reliance upon those around her who understood the laws and had her best interest at heart.

LET every soul be subject to the higher powers. For there is no power but of God: the powers that be are ordained of God. Whosoever therefore resists the power, resists the ordinance of God: and they that resist shall receive to themselves damnation.

—Romans 13:1-2 KJVER

After doing a word study, I created this paraphrase: Choose to put yourself under those who are superior in ability and influence, those assigned and appointed by God, and then refuse any opposition or you will receive judgment against yourself.[11] The key is to submit to those assigned and appointed by God. Ruth placed herself under those who were of great ability and influence, superior in their understanding of the laws and customs of the land, appointed by God. And she obeyed them.

The Providence of God

God's providential footsteps can be seen throughout the story of Ruth. Once she made the decision to embrace Naomi's God, she was divinely guided to the field of Naomi's relative. Because of Ruth's humble, submissive attitude toward Naomi, God's favor was poured out upon her through Boaz. He not only invited her to stay in his field and glean, but she was given extra privileges of picking up more of the harvest, eating at His table and drinking water with his employees.

God divinely placed people in Ruth's life, like the young maidens, to direct her steps and teach her His ways. The process of Ruth's experience was divinely ordered as well. At first, her relationship with her redeemer was from a distance. Then, he was a casual acquaintance. The next level brought her to his feet. Then she married Him. This provides a picture of what Jesus wants for us. God even divinely worked out Ruth's "business" through Boaz at the "place of judgment." Ruth went through training, testing, preparation, and intimacy—all under the tutelage of the Lord.

Co-Laborer in Preparation for Christ

Naomi advised Ruth to do specific things in preparation for her security for redemption and marriage. She was told to wash and anoint herself, put her mantle on, and get down to the threshing floor. Once at the threshing floor, she was to wait until Boaz had finished eating and drinking before she made herself known. When he lay down, she was to mark the place where he would lie, go in and uncover his feet, lie down and listen to what he would tell her to do. This passage is full of incredible spiritual significance.

After doing a word study, I believe this passage lays out the believer's preparation for redemption and marriage: washing through the water of the Word (water baptism), anointing through the smearing of the oil (Spirit baptism), putting on Christ, and getting to the place of crushing (death to self).[12] At the place of crushing, the disciple of Christ can become more intimate with the Lord because he/she can identify with Him in His death and operate from a place of His resurrection power.

Another layer of understanding in this passage is the process that Jesus went through to gain our redemption. Ruth was to wait until Boaz was finished eating and drinking before she made herself known. Likewise, Jesus had his last Passover meal with his disciples before He was taken to the Garden of Gethsemane. It was after Jesus was apprehended that the disciples fled and denied that they knew Him, consequently, making their true selves known. Boaz's lying down could represent Christ's crucifixion, death, and burial. When his feet are uncovered, he symbolizes Christ enabling us to be the dwelling place for the Holy Spirit as He tells us what to do.

The Law Verses Grace

The law was never meant to redeem men, but only lead us to a Savior.

> Therefore by the deeds of the law there shall no flesh be justified in His sight: for by the law is the knowledge of sin.
>
> —Romans 3:20 KJVER

> Being justified freely by His grace through the redemption that is in Christ Je´sus.
>
> —Romans 3:24 KJVER

Boaz went to the city gate (the place where judgment and business transactions were conducted) on behalf of Ruth, just as Jesus did for mankind. He satisfied the requirements of the law by giving the nearer kinsman an opportunity to fulfill his obligation. The nearer kinsman could take care of the family's property/land, but could not fulfill Ruth's needs. What Boaz did for Ruth is a beautiful picture of what Jesus did as taught in the New Testament.

> For the law of the Spirit of life in Christ Je′sus has made me free from the law of sin and death. For what the law could not do, in that it was weak through the flesh, God sending His own Son in the likeness of sinful flesh, and for sin, condemned sin in the flesh: That the righteousness of the law might be fulfilled in us, who walk not after the flesh, but after the Spirit.
>
> —Romans 8:2-4 KJVER

The nearer kinsman only looked after that which fulfilled the law, making no room for grace, thus Boaz stepped in to fully redeem that which was lost.

> For the law made nothing perfect, but the bringing in of a better hope *did*; by the which we draw near to God.
>
> —Hebrews 7:19 KJVER

Personal Decisions Affect Many Generations

Ruth had no idea what the future ramifications were when she told Naomi that she would follow her wherever she went, embracing her people and her God for a lifetime. Her commitment reverberated through ten generations of those needing restoration to enter into the congregation of the Lord. Her forefathers had committed sinful acts and it was Ruth who brought back what was lost. Her generation also began anew, and it was through her seed that David and, eventually, Jesus were birthed (Ruth 4:17-22, Matthew 1:1-17, Genesis 38:12-30).

True Redemption

I had been studying the subject of salvation, "being saved", and eternal life for several weeks since going out on the streets with a team of leaders to evangelize the lost. This "evangelistic event" came to the Cincinnati area and I wanted to be a part of seeing people come to the Lord. However, I was disenchanted with how salvation was promoted and wanted to hear from the Lord what the scriptures say in regards to salvation and true redemption. And then, the Lord reminded me that I was studying the book of Ruth and that those four chapters contained a perfect example of what redemption really looks like.

The character of Ruth is a perfect model of redemption for the believer who walks by faith and not by sight. Naomi (representing the Jews, the religious) is a model of God's plan of redemption for those who walk by circumstances and unbelief. And Boaz is God's example of Jesus, our true Redeemer. The characters in the book of Ruth are symbolic and necessary for understanding God's plan of redemption, but the understanding I gleaned from the book itself has convinced me that redemption encompasses so much more.

Ruth made several choices that would change her life forever. She left her family, land, and people to embrace God. She walked away from Moab (her wash pot or garbage dump) and chose to follow Naomi's God with total abandon. She had no ulterior motives. She was completely committed to her God, knowing that she would probably never marry or have children and would be giving her life to serve her beloved mother-in-law, Naomi.

Ruth remained in the field where the young maidens were, choosing not to be distracted by the young men (nothing took first place in her heart). She partook of the food and drink that was given her in the field that was provided by Boaz (she was fed by Him). She took Naomi's advice by taking responsibility for her cleansing (washing of the water through the Word), for her anointing (death to the flesh through the work of the Holy Spirit) and for her putting on the proper garment

(His righteousness) in preparation for marriage. She then went down to the threshing floor—a place of humility, sacrifice, purging, and even warring—healing and deliverance. The process of redemption was deliberate on God's part and Ruth continued to have an attitude of submission and obedience that brought her to the feet of her very Redeemer.

God's redemption is complete for all men. Naomi represents God's chosen people. She knows the rules governing her people but seeks to find salvation and deliverance on her own. The Bible says that the wages of sin is death (Romans 6:23). Naomi's husband, Elimelech, experienced death prematurely after seeking food in a foreign land rather than remaining in the "House of Bread" and trusting that God would provide, even though there was a severe famine.

Her sons, Mahlon and Chilion, remained in the place of spiritual death and joined themselves with foreign wives without any intentions of returning to their homeland. And Naomi became bitter toward God because of the deaths of those she loved the most. Thankfully, God did not give up on Naomi. He still wooed her regardless of her beliefs about Him. God used the most unlikely candidate, her surrendered daughter-in-law, to draw her back to Himself through love. God kept His promise made to Abraham by preserving fallen-man's ability to return to a place of His presence and by protecting the bloodline so that a Savior would be born.

God's plan of redemption for all mankind moved from the law, and when the law could not redeem, God sent His Kinsman Redeemer that not only fulfilled the law, but went above and beyond the law's intentions. Boaz is a perfect type and foreshadowing of Jesus. He embraces man and places him in His field with all the provisions necessary to grow into maturity. He takes notice of man's heart, devotion, and desire to follow hard after Him and rewards him with His grace and favor. He invites man to His banqueting table to partake of Him. He lays down His life at the threshing floor where robbers come to steal and sleep is scarce—it's a place of hardship. He affirms His covenant with man by becoming man's advocate at the city gate (place of judgment). The law (outward acts, religion, and the traditions of men) is not able to redeem man, only Jesus can fully redeem man.

The book of Ruth is full of spiritual lessons on true redemption. Ruth commits herself to God completely and is given full benefits in God's kingdom. Naomi who is walking in unbelief is shown God's heart of provision and grace through Ruth, the converted one. And Boaz, Jesus, walks among His own and serves the purposes of God on earth so that all mankind can be fully redeemed and restored. True redemption cannot be reduced to a simple emotional prayer if it is not coupled with total surrender, submission, and obedience—not just for a moment, but for a lifetime. We cannot be redeemed through the law, religion, or even who we know, unless the person we truly know is Jesus. And then we must abide with Him in His field and on His threshing floor, with complete and total trust until our marriage union is complete. This is true redemption.

Are you an Orpah, Ruth, or a Naomi?

You and I fit into one of three categories of people in the book of Ruth: (1) An Orpah—someone who bases life's decisions on the temporal and the natural mind, thus, remaining in bondage, with no opportunity for restoration unless a decision is made to leave the old and embrace the new. (2) A Ruth—someone who walks by faith, not by sight and is committed unconditionally to following Christ at whatever the cost, (3) A Naomi—someone who is stuck in life's adversities, suffering from an identity crisis, and unable to live the abundant life in its fullness, subject to God's mercy and grace for full restoration through someone else's blessings.

God was actively involved in Orpah's life even though she lived in a foreign, pagan country with an ungodly upbringing. She was exposed to the truth by God's grace when she married into Naomi's family. She had just as much opportunity to follow Naomi's God as Ruth did.

However, she opted to return to the "comforts" of home and what she knew from her past. Orpah thought it was more important to work out her life the way it suited her best. She was limited to what she could see with the natural mind.

In the same way, God was actively involved in Ruth's life through the life of Naomi. Have you wondered why Ruth would lay everything down and follow Naomi with such abandon? God was obviously working in Ruth's heart long before she made the choice to embrace Him. Because of her unconditional commitment, He led her to the field of provision, showed her grace and favor, and encouraged her to remain amongst those who would keep her pure. She was comforted, shown hospitality, and given key insights that would lead her to the place of intimacy. Boaz (Jesus) went to the place of judgment for her and purchased her so that the generations after her could also be made spiritually alive. He gave her back what was lost—her husband, a child, and hope for the future.

And finally, God was actively involved in the life of Naomi. He had not given up on her even though she saw Him as harsh and judgmental and had given up on any hope of a future. He loved her so much that He provided her with someone who would restore all that was lost—a family, a sense of purpose, provision, an inheritance, and truth about who God is. God worked behind the scenes, restoring life back to Naomi.

Which one do you identify with—Orpah, Ruth, or Naomi? If you are an Orpah but you want to be a Ruth, will you lay down all your hopes and dreams, and leave your place of bondage and walk by faith, knowing that God is sovereign and makes all things new again? Will you refuse the wash pots in your life and step into the place of provision? Are you willing to embrace God at whatever the cost and believe what He says about you? Will you identify with Him today rather than relate to Him based upon your past?

If you are a Naomi, will you trust the Lord by seeking Him regardless of your circumstances, knowing that His grace is sufficient for you?

Will you dare to put into practice what the Word says about God and yourself, and live out of God's truth? Will you get God's perspective by going to the top where He dwells and refuse to associate with a victim mentality? Will you re-identify yourself with whom God says you are and refuse the lies of the enemy?

If you can identify with Ruth, will you complete the journey that God has you on and devote your heart, mind, and soul to the things that will keep you pure? Will you stay away from the "young men" and refuse the distractions so that you can keep yourself washed, anointed, and clothed with Christ? Will you learn obedience by the things that you suffer and lay down your life so that Christ can live through you? Will you become intimate with the Father by learning to listen and hearken diligently to His voice so that when a famine hits, you will know how to receive your provision? Will you submit to the authorities God has ordained in your life and be used of God in the lives of the Naomi's of the world?

Regardless of which one you relate to, God is still working on your behalf. He wants to know you intimately and be known by you. He longs to fill you up with all His fullness. He longs to share secrets with you and train you in His Word so that you can discern good and evil. It is your destiny to see His hand in your life as you walk along the way—not as a taskmaster but a lover. You are here on earth to fulfill the destiny and purposes of God in this generation and to see future generations experience Him too. Will you allow Him to re-direct your future and the future of those who come after you?

I began this study with a look at why it is vital that we nurture the Seed that is in us and ended with Ruth's story of redemption. Our relationship with God is not something that just happens in a moment. We need Him for a lifetime. We can never know it all or have enough of the Lord. He is infinite, always unfolding more of Himself. God promises an abundant life through knowing His voice and following Him (John 10:10). We have an inheritance in Him (Ephesians 1:17-23).

It is my prayer, as Paul said it best,

That He would grant you, according to the riches of His glory, to be
strengthened with might by His Spirit in the inner man; That Christ
may dwell in your hearts by faith; that you, being rooted and grounded
in love, May be able to comprehend with all saints what *is* the breadth,
and length, and depth, and height; And to know the love of Christ,
which passes knowledge, that you might be filled with all the fullness
of God. Now to Him that is able to do exceeding abundantly above
all that we ask or think, according to the power that works in us. To
Him *be* glory in the church by Christ Jes´us throughout all ages, world
without end. Amen.

—Ephesians 3:16-21 KJVER

So be it, Lord.

Chapter 10

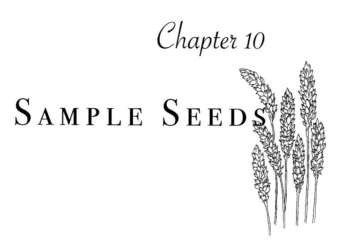

SAMPLE SEEDS

Please note: the following words and their meanings have been taken from *Strong's Exhaustive Concordance of the Bible* by James Strong and the other information was gleaned from either the *King James Easy-Reading Study Bible* or *The New Unger's Bible Dictionary* by Merrill F. Unger.

Disclaimer: This Bible study is meant to encourage you, the student, to seek the Lord for His truth. My sample seeds are given so that you have an idea of what I am looking for. However, my answers are up for debate. As you pray and seek the Holy Spirit for knowledge and wisdom, and use the true plumb line of God's Word, it is my hope that you will become a Berean (Acts 17:10-11) as the scriptures admonish.

Chapter One

Section B

Famine (7458) – hunger, dearth; Moab (4124) – an incestuous son of Lot, "from father"; Bethlehem-Judah (1035) – "House of Bread"; Elimelech (458) – "God of the King"; Naomi (5281) – "pleasant"; Mahlon (4248) – "sick"; Chilion (3630) – "wasting away"; Orpah (6204) – neck, stiff-necked; Ruth (7327) – "friend"; Mara (4755) – "bitter."[13]

Section C

1. Naomi's situation is so grievous that she equates who she is with what her situation has become. Naomi means "pleasant" and Mara means "bitter."[14] She is unable to hope or believe for anything more than what her circumstances have dictated.

2. She told her daughters-in-law three times to return. Orpah finally did, and then, Naomi tried to convince Ruth a fourth time, but Ruth refused. The number three means to conform, imitate, obey; four means to rule and reign.[15] Orpah would be conforming to the ways she knew, and Ruth would be stepping into a higher level of authority.

Section D

1. Its origins come from an incestuous relationship between Lot and his daughter. God calls Moab His wash pot or garbage dump in Psalm 108:9. Moab (5518, 7366) – a hook, caldron, fishhook, to boil up a pot, a bath.[16] A place for someone to be cleansed. God certainly uses Moab to bring judgment to Israel. In Genesis 19:34-38, Lot's daughters got him drunk and slept with him. They both became pregnant. The firstborn bore him a son and called him Moab (the father of the Moabites). In Numbers 25:1-5 they were a snare to the Israelites. In 1 Samuel 22:3-4 David found refuge from his mom and dad in Moab.

2. In the days when there was no king in Israel, men did what was right in their own eyes; therefore, judges were set in place and regions were governed separately rather than as a whole. There was a cycle that kept repeating itself during this time period: Jews did evil → were sold to their enemies → cried to God in trouble → a deliverer was raised up → there was a period of rest → people sinned again. This left the Israelites easy prey for idolatrous influences. The judges acted as divine agents of God's will.[17]

3. He was a man of the tribe of Judah who dwelt in Bethlehem-Judah in the days of the judges. Judah – When Judah first went into Egypt, he

had three sons, but it increases in size to the greatest (76,500) – numbered first amongst all the tribes. Place – positioned on the east side of the Tabernacle toward the sunrise. During the rule of the judges, Judah was independent of the other tribes. Judah's personal history – Judah's advice sold Joseph into slavery rather than have him killed. His son married Tamar and died, second son married her and died, and Judah withheld his third son so Tamar tricked Judah. She acted like a prostitute, lured Judah and was impregnated by him – she bore Zerah and Perez (Pharez). Judah was the fourth son of Jacob and Leah.[18]

Section E

1.   No, the reason they went there was to find food – there was a famine in the land. In verse 1, the word *sojourn* (1481) means as a guest, be a stranger, turn aside from the road.[19]

2.   Her two sons married two Moabite women.

3.   Orpah – she stayed a time and followed Naomi until she was convinced that there would be no husband, inheritance, children, or future. Ruth – she went with Naomi without any "benefits" because she loved Naomi and wanted to embrace Naomi's God. She was willing to give up her life for another. There were no ulterior motives.

4.   Naomi had heard there was food in her land and that God had visited her people.

> And Na-o´mi said unto her two daughters in law, Go, return each to her mother's house: the LORD deal kindly with you, as you have dealt with the dead, and with me. The LORD grant you that you may find rest, each *of you* in the house of her husband. Then she kissed them; and they lifted up their voice, and wept.
> —Ruth 1:8-9 KJVER

In other words, she wanted them to marry a man from their people, have children, and prosper. Naomi had nothing to offer them. She had no more sons nor was there opportunity to bear more children and wait several years for them to grow up so they could re-marry. It was a dead-end for them. As far as she was concerned, there was nothing more she could do for them.

5. Her blessing: God treats Orpah and Ruth the same way that they have treated Naomi and that they find security by getting married and settling down.

6. Orpah's commitment was based on her current circumstances and her reasoning. Ruth's commitment was based on her love for Naomi and her God.

7. Ruth didn't care about her future security. She was more concerned that Naomi was taken care of. She chose to work the fields to support Naomi rather than to go back to her land and people and look out for herself. On top of that, Ruth embraced Naomi's land, people, faith, and her God.

8. It was the beginning of barley season, so it was in early April. Barley is used for bread for the very poor (2 Kings 4:42). It was part of the price of an adulteress (Hos. 3:2) and of lewd women (Ezek. 13:19) and showed the low rank and poverty of Gideon (Judges 7:13). Barley is earlier than the wheat harvest (Ex. 9:31-32).[20]

9. No, they didn't recognize her. It had been at least ten years, and maybe many more, since she had been in Bethlehem. She probably had aged from all the stress of losing her husband and two sons and concerning herself with how she would provide for herself.

10. Naomi had lost her husband and two sons. She thought God was judging and afflicting her.

Section F

1. God still allows man free will, but His hand is always involved in the affairs of men. He lets people know His doings.

Section G

1. I would not move. This shows a lack of trust. I would press into the Lord in prayer, fasting and repentance for our land. Famine is an indicator of judgment (Lev. 26:26-27, Psa. 105:16, Lam. 4:4,6, Ezek. 14:21). See Deut. 28. Causes of famine – 1. God's blessings withheld (Hos. 2:8-9; Hag. 1:6). 2. Seed rot (Amos 4:9; Hag. 2:17). 3. Pestilence (Ezek. 7:15; Matt. 24:7).[21]

2. No, in Neh. 13:23-27, the Jews married foreign women, who worshipped other gods, causing the Jews to sin. This was Solomon's and Samson's downfall. It is not the fact that they are foreigners, but that they worshipped other gods.

> Be you not unequally yoked together with unbelievers: for what fellowship has righteousness with unrighteousness? and what communion has light with darkness?
>
> —2 Corinthians 6:14 KJVER

We are to be separate (Joshua 9, Deut. 6:14, Deut. 22:10, Deut. 7:3-4).

Section I

1. In Mosaic Law, the Jews couldn't marry the Canaanites because it would lead them to idolatry (Ex. 34:15-16; Deut. 7:3-4). The Moabite men could not marry Israelite women, but the Israelite men could marry Moabite women.[22]

2. Naomi is a type of Jew and Ruth is a type of Gentile. God's mystery of the one new man is recognizable in the book of Ruth. God uses the Jews to bring in the Gentiles, and then, He uses the Gentiles to provoke the Jews to jealousy. His plan is for the one new man and the love and friendship between the two to bring about God's purposes on earth. This understanding will accomplish great things. We need each other.

There are truths that the Gentiles do not know or understand that come from the Jews' understanding of the law. And, there are blessings/provisions that we have that the Jews need in order to see God's hand once again.

Chapter Two

Section B

Kinsman (1350) – to buy back a relative's property, marry his widow, redeem, next of kin; grace (2580) – graciousness, kindness, beauty, well-favored; sheaves (6016) – a dry measure, a heap; stranger (5237) – strange, non-relative, different; trust (2620) – to flee for protection, to confide in, have hope, make refuge; favor (2580) – same as grace above; lord (113) – to rule, sovereign, owner, master; purpose (7997) – to drop or strip, to plunder, let fall; sufficed (7646) – fill to satisfaction; maidens (5291) – a girl from infancy to adolescence.[23]

Section C

1. Both Boaz and Naomi were protecting young Ruth from a lesser destiny—meeting a young man her age and being distracted from not only marriage, a son, but true redemption. The story accentuates this so that the learner can be aware of God's perfect will and that our choices do matter. Even though she wasn't convinced at first, she obeyed. It was another test to lay down the flesh and follow God.

2. Wings (3671) – an edge or extremity, corner, end; trust (2620) – to flee for protection, to confide in, have hope, make refuge. Ruth places herself in the safety of Naomi's God without any benefits. His arms are outstretched to include her because of her "hope in Him."[24]

3. Bread – figurative of the body of Jesus; vinegar – figurative of the blood of Jesus. This story beautifully illustrates our need to lay all down, follow Him without ulterior motives, partake of Him, and receive what He has done for true redemption. We are to partake of

Him and allow the flesh to die, receive the forgiveness of sin, and live a resurrected life.

Section D

1. "Coming to help or rescue" – go´el – nearest living male blood relative – avenger. Redeemer – redeem the paternal estate that his nearest relative might have sold through poverty, to act as go-between for restitution. It is not normally the responsibility of the kinsman redeemer to marry the widow (this obligation is limited to a brother according to the Levirate law). The nearest kinsman had the right to redeem the land which could include marrying the widow of the deceased owner.[25]

2. When the grain was cut, it was gathered on the arms, bound in sheaves, and laid in heaps to be threshed. The corners of the fields were not reaped and the gleanings of the fields were left to the poor (Lev. 19:9, Deut. 24:19, Deut. 23:25). The Israelites passing along the field were allowed to pluck the heads of the ripened grain left in the field. A handful of purpose is a deliberate dropping rather than picking up the leftovers. In other words, Boaz gave Ruth permission to gather the first fruits rather than from the leftovers. The sheaves were the bundles already cut.[26]

Section E

1. Ruth did not know who Boaz was nor did Naomi tell her. This demonstrates God's hand in directing her to the right field because she chose to trust Him.

2. Boaz did not know her personally but had only heard about her.

3. He instructed her to stay in his field amongst the young maidens. He also gave her permission to drink from his water source.

4.   He learned of Ruth's kindness toward Naomi, that she was a widow and how she had left her homeland and her family and had come to a people she did not know.

5.   Grace and favor are defined the same in the concordance. He doesn't withhold from them that walk uprightly (Psa. 84:11). According to the Bible Dictionary, "grace is what God is free to do." Favor means God doesn't hold back and He is deliberate about directing our paths. It is contingent upon our obedience though (Job 42:10). Job prayed for his friends and God restored double. It is interesting that Ruth asks Boaz why she has found grace in his eyes and then asks for favor in his sight. The key words are eyes and sight. The word eyes implies something that comes from Boaz and sight implies something Boaz sees in Ruth. In other words, Ruth would like to change from within – experience a heart change.

6.   He instructed them to not bother Ruth. He also asked them to allow her to glean among that which had already been cut and bundled. This was above what the law required.

7.   An ephah of barley is three pints or five days worth. A handful of purpose is that which was dropped deliberately and could fit in a human hand.[27]

8.   Naomi discovered that Ruth was gleaning on a relative's land. She blessed Boaz for being an instrument of God's kindness to those who had died and those who remained. She knew God was taking care of her and Ruth through the kinsman-redeemer's law.

9.   She told Ruth it was good to stay with the young maidens in Boaz's field.

Section F

1.   God directs the path of those who are fully following Him. He also honors those who abandon all to follow Him with favor, grace, provision,

redemption, etc. God looks after His people—those who have lost their way and those who are grafted in.

Section G

1. Listen, stay close to those who are mature in the Lord, learn from them, avoid those who would pull me away and keep myself full of the Holy Spirit. Partake of Him fully.

2. He uses Ruth (Gentiles grafted in) and Boaz (Jesus) to bring Naomi (Jews) back into the fold. This is a prophetic act of what God is doing for the Jews who are feeling afflicted, forsaken, and bitter. God is good at restoring those who are disengaged and disheartened.

Section I

1. The Lord's Supper – "a meal belonging to the Lord." This is a meal instituted by Jesus while observing the Passover with His disciples.

> And as they were eating, Je′sus took bread, and blessed *it*, and broke *it*, and gave *it* to the disciples, and said, Take, eat; this is My body. And He took the cup, and gave thanks, and gave *it* to them, saying, Drink you all of it; For this is My blood of the new testament, which is shed for many for the remission of sins.
> —Matthew 26:26-28 KJVER

Paul teaches about partaking of the body (bread=death) and cup (blood=Life), symbolic of death to the flesh and newness of life.

> And when He had given thanks, He broke it, and said, Take, eat: this is My body, which is broken for you: this do in remembrance of Me. After the same manner also He *took* the cup, when He had supped, saying, This cup is the new testament in My blood: this do you, as often as you drink *it*, in remembrance of Me. For as often as you eat this bread, and drink this cup, you do show the Lord's death till He come.
> —1 Cor. 11:24-26 KJVER

We are further admonished to drink the cup and eat the bread worthily so that we are not guilty of killing the Lord. In other words, we are to fully partake of Him. We are to examine ourselves so that we are not judged. Many are sick and weak and asleep because they don't heed this admonition. This practice has more to do with dealing with sin, allowing the flesh to die, and receiving forgiveness than it does with the act itself. It also has to do with intimacy, relationship, and partaking of Jesus completely rather than following laws, rules, and being religious.

2. Jesus came to rescue us. The law was the nearest kin, but it couldn't satisfy our need to be purchased, so Jesus, the perfect Lamb, was sacrificed in our place (for the wages of sin is death, Romans 6:23). He chose to fulfill the law and redeem us from the curse of death so that we could have relationship with our Father. He was fully man and therefore could avenge us by His blood, but He was also fully God, therefore sinless. Jesus is also planning a marriage feast and a wedding for His Bride, the church. Jesus purchased the world, buying back all from Satan's kingdom when He died for us.

Chapter Three

Section B

Rest (in verse 1) - (4494) – quiet, a settled spot, a home, a place of rest (in verse 18) – (8252) – to repose, appease, idleness, be still; wash (7364) – to bathe self; anoint (5480) – to smear over with oil; mark or notice (3045) – to know, ascertain by seeing, make self known; virtuous (2428) – a force, an army, valor, strength, substance, worthy.[28]

Section C

1. She was seeking a home for her – security, provision, a new life.

2. 1. Wash yourself. 2. Anoint yourself. 3. Put on your best garments.

Our preparation for marriage to our Bride groom is to be changed from the inside out. The Holy Spirit's job is to convict us of sin, and we are to cleanse ourselves by obedience to the Word. We are to receive power from on High and put on Christ (His nature, fruit, gifts, etc.).

3.   Near kinsman – Jesus; Nearer Kinsman – the law; the law was meant to lead us to Jesus, the fulfillment of the law. The six measures of barley represent man and may have been a sign to Naomi that Boaz was taking care of Ruth (man was created on the sixth day).

4.   Naomi was asking Ruth what took place because she looks different. Something had changed.

5.   I believe Boaz's provision of six measures of barley was an indicator to Naomi that he was taking care of Ruth, since the number six is the number of man.

Section D

1.   The uncovering of the feet was a mark of adoration and the covering of the feet was performing the necessities of nature. To cover with a skirt is a token of matrimony. The threshing floor represents chastisement, crushing, labor, judgment, separation of good and bad—a place to crush the flesh. This is a picture of what is needed to enter into the kingdom—submission, humility, adoration, a forsaking of the flesh, and total acceptance of Him.[29]

2.   The nearer kinsman represents the current covenant—the law. But the law could not redeem man it was only there to show man his need for One greater. The One who could/would receive a foreigner into the fold who laid it all down for Him. The law only dealt with rules and judgments, not the redemption of people.

Section E

1. Ruth agreed to do all that Naomi told her to do.

2. He was guarding the harvest from thieves.[30]

3. He proclaimed a blessing over her because she did not seek after a young man who would only satisfy her short-term needs. She allowed full redemption, God's way.

4. She did not want to be seen by others. The text implies that it was not a common practice to have a woman at the threshing floor. Could this be prophetic of the rapture?

Section F

1. God works within His law, but He also makes up for what the law cannot do. God follows through with all the details associated with man's needs. He cares for all those involved. Even those who are embittered by what life has dealt them.

2. God makes sure man's needs are satisfied. He honors those who give their all to Him. He leads by example: death to the flesh, resurrection life, and ascension—something we will experience in its fullness.

Section G

1. We need each other. The Jews have an understanding of the law that the Gentiles can glean from and the Jews need to see God's hand through the Gentiles' provision.

2. Man lays down all—land, people family, hopes, his dreams, and embraces God. This includes having a humble and obedient servant's attitude. There is much testing, tribulation, and separating that takes place to get man to the place of true readiness for the wedding.

Section I

1. Grain was cut with a sickle and gathered on the arms bound in sheaves and laid in heaps to be threshed. Threshing floors were in the

open air on elevated grounds—the wheat was trampled and then thrown up in the air so that the chaff may be carried away. The grain was then sifted. God prepares us for Him. We are to be pure. This takes much threshing and sifting.[31]

2. Six (8337) – a surplus beyond five or the fingers of the hand; measure (374) – ephah. According to the Bible dictionary in metrology, an ephah contained ten omers (three pecks and three pints)—a daily food allowance times six. Six – six days of creation, man created on the sixth day, six days labor and man's work is done—God's will be done.[32]

Chapter Four

Section B

Gate (8179) – an opening, city door; redeem (1350) – next of kin and buy back a relative's property and marry his widow; mar (7843) – to decay, ruin, batter, cast off, corrupt, destroy; witnesses (5707) – testimony, a recorder; purchased (7069) – to erect, create, procure by purchase, to own, recover, redeem; restorer (7725) – to turn back, to retreat, recover, refresh; nourisher (3557) – to keep in, to maintain, feed, provide sustenance; Obed – "serving."[33]

Section C

1. God uses this story to show us how the law cannot redeem man. The law is limited; it can only lead us to Christ. Jesus fulfilled the law.

2. Make Ruth like Rachel and Leah – twelve offspring. Build the house of Israel—a prophecy for those who would believe. Prosper in Ephrathah and be famous in Bethlehem – Jesus was born in Bethlehem. This is a prophecy about Jesus. House be like the house of Pharez – Tamar. She was grafted in and produced children with Judah to continue the bloodline. The Gentiles were grafted in and continue to fulfill the prophecy of offspring who walk by faith and are justified like Abraham.

3. The number seven means completeness, fullness, all, finished.[34] Sons (1121) – a builder of the family name, nation, anointed one, quality or condition, arranged. Ruth is being compared to being better than the fullest family because she birthed no ordinary child. She carries the bloodline of Jesus.[35]

Section D

1. In Deuteronomy 25:5-10 the wife of the dead is not to marry outside the family. She is to marry the husband's brother. Her firstborn shall take the name of the dead so that his name continues. If the brother does not want to take the brother's wife, she must go to the gate of the elders and tell them of his refusal. The elders are to call him, and she is to come to him in the elder's presence and take off his shoe, spit in his face and say, "so shall it be done to that man that will not build up his brother's house." He shall be called in Israel, "The house of him that has his shoe loosed."

2. Rachel and Leah were sisters. Jacob worked for seven years for Rachel, but got Leah and then had to work seven more years for Rachel (Gen. 29). Leah was able to conceive, but Rachel could not for many years. At one point she gave her maid to Jacob in order to secure children (Gen. 30:3-4). Leah bore four sons and Rachel became jealous and then gave the maid to him. Bilhah conceived two sons. Then Leah gave Jacob her maid and she bore two more sons. Leah bore two more sons and one daughter. Rachel finally conceived and bore Joseph and then Benjamin, but she died in childbirth in Bethlehem. Jacob had twelve sons, building God's government.

3. Judah had two ungodly sons. The firstborn married Tamar, but died. Then Judah gave Tamar his brother to carry on the family name. He died as well. Tamar was promised Judah's third son, but Judah held him back, so Tamar dressed up like a prostitute and tricked Judah. Judah impregnated Tamar with twins. The one who came out first was Pharez.

Pharez is mentioned in the genealogy of Jesus. Just as Tamar was grafted in, so was Ruth.

4. There's ten generations from Pharez to David. There is significance to the passing of ten generations.

> **HE** that is wounded in the stones or has his privy member cut off, shall not enter into the congregation of the LORD. An illegitimate child shall not enter into the congregation of the LORD; even to his tenth generation shall he not enter into the congregation of the LORD. An Am´mon-ite or Mo´ab-ite shall not enter into the congregation of the LORD; even to their tenth generation shall they not enter into the congregation of the LORD forever.
>
> —Deuteronomy 23:1-3 KJVER

So, from Pharez to David is ten generations which infers a new day—entry into the congregation of the Lord.

Section E

1. According to *Understanding the Dreams You Dream* by Ira Milligan, the number ten symbolizes measure for the purpose of accepting or rejecting that which is measured.[36] In this case the nearer kinsman was rejecting Boaz's offer to redeem the land and Ruth, and the kinsman, Boaz, was accepting his responsibility in front of the ten elders.

2. Marriage was not required but was considered a duty of love. This is a beautiful foreshadowing of what the law could not do and what Jesus did out of true love.

3. He felt it would taint his own inheritance. Maybe he would have to share his inheritance with more offspring through Ruth and he didn't want to spread out his wealth.

4. Could this be figurative in the sense that Naomi (Israel) is restored and will embrace God's Son? Could it possibly be prophetic of Israel's

future, realizing who Jesus is? Finally, Israel's eyes are opened and they embrace their Messiah?

5.   They announced that Naomi had bore a son and named him Obed (servant). First of all, Ruth bore Obed, but she's out of the picture. Was this prophetic of the Gentile age being over? The Israelites receive the Messiah as servant and the Church Age is over?

6.   There are ten generations.

7.   Jesus was born and is famous in Bethlehem—a foreshadowing of the coming Messiah.

Section F

1.   He spoke blessings over his servants and Ruth. He gave above and beyond the law. He knows the law, follows it, but also knows how to uphold it and fulfill it. He goes to great lengths to provide for his own. He doesn't look out for Himself but for others.

2.   The law could not redeem man, only property. The law has limitations on what it can do. It is not flexible.

Section G

1.   We need each other. Ruth was used in Naomi's life to restore her hope in God. Naomi was used in Ruth's life to teach her the law and guide her to her destiny in God more fully.

Section I

1.   The Levirate Law is explained in Deuteronomy 25:5-10 and is a law to protect the family name, carry on the bloodline and provide for the widow.

2.   In Deuteronomy 23:1-3 the law states that if a half breed enters into the marriage covenant they cannot enter into the congregation of the Lord, even an Ammonite or Moabite. Because of what Tamar and

Judah did (had an illicit relationship out of trickery, father-in-law with daughter-in-law), beginning with Pharez, the ten generations that followed were excluded from God's presence until the tenth generation, which was David. This just shows God's redemptive grace toward man. And Jesus came through this bloodline.

EPILOGUE

AFTER MY MONTHS' long study of the book of Ruth, the Lord has made it clear to me that ***Ruth: Road to Redemption*** is not just another Bible study to be sold, studied, and set on a shelf—it represents His anointing on those who would take Ruth's mantle and cling to the "Naomi's" of the world who are embittered by their circumstances and in desperate need of love, grace, and provision.

This revelation was defined when God shared with me that this mantle had been placed upon me. This explains the burden I have had for those in prison, families who have been torn apart by divorce and murder, and loved ones who have embraced a lifestyle of drug/alcohol/ food addictions. It confirms why my heart is torn for homosexuals, the promiscuous, the young children and women who are abused and used in the slave and sex trafficking market, and to the unwed women who are struggling to provide for themselves and their babies. This further clarifies the burden I have for those who have not come into their full destiny and purpose in God and who are blinded and unable to see who God truly is.

God is passionate about reversing the injustices in our world and saving His people from the snare of the enemy. There are ministries that are touching lives in these ways, such as:

- *The Shepherd's Crook*, a ministry that is rescuing the unwanted orphans of the world.
- *In the Cleft of the Rock Ministries International*, a ministry to the Jews, with a commitment to seeing God's people fully walk in His plan and purpose for their lives.
- *The Rocking Chair*, a ministry that takes in unwed mothers and babies and ministers to the whole person, just to name a few.
- Missionaries who are not just going into a culture and Americanizing the people groups, but are living in such a way that lives are being changed forever.

Sadly, in many cases, I find ministries barely making ends meet and the dedicated ones burning out because of a lack of funds. Our society in its entrepreneurial pursuits has almost completely forgotten the mandate to feed the poor and minister to the widows and orphans—something God calls, true religion. When this is done to the least of these, it is done unto Him. These ministries and many like them must be funded and supported in prayer.

Just like Ruth who sacrificially gleaned after the reapers in the grain fields so that she and Naomi could eat and fulfill the destiny and purpose of God, so must we sacrificially give to restore God's justice to the earth. One way to do this is to give to: *Into the Highways and Hedges*—a ministry that the Lord is establishing (all the proceeds of this book, minus expenses and a minimum salary go back into the work of the Lord) to support ministries that are reaching out to the "Naomi's" of the world. If you want more information, please contact me, Terri Lustig, at (513) 783-7723 or go to my website: www.intothehighwaysandhedges.com.

Appendix I

CHAPTER OUTLINES AND TITLE SUMMATIONS

Chapter One – "Famine & Death"

There is a famine in the land of Bethlehem-Judah during the time when the judges ruled. Elimelech, Naomi, and their two sons go to Moab. Elimelech dies in Moab and Naomi's two sons take Moabite women as their wives and live in Moab ten more years.

Both sons die and once Naomi hears that the famine is over in Bethelehem-Judah, she makes the decision to go back to her hometown. She tells her two daughters-in-law to return to their own families so they can find a husband who can provide for them. She kisses them and leaves. They weep and insist on going with Naomi. Naomi tries to convince them to return because she has no more sons who can be their husbands and bear their children. They weep again.

After three requests, Orpah kisses Naomi goodbye, but Ruth clings to Naomi. Naomi tries to convince Ruth to return to Moab a fourth time, but Ruth will not leave her.

And Ruth said, Entreat me not to leave you, *or* to return from following after you: for where you go, I will go; and where you lodge, I will lodge: your people *shall be* my people, and your God, *my* God: Where you die, will I die, and there will I be buried: the LORD do so to me, and more also, if *anything* but death part you and me.

—Ruth 1:16-17 KJVER

Naomi gives up trying to convince Ruth to stay in Moab. They finally leave Moab and go to Bethlehem-Judah. On their way, the people are unsure of Naomi's appearance. Naomi wants to be called "Mara" instead of Naomi. It is the beginning of barley harvest.

Chapter Two – "Training Camp"

Naomi has a kinsman of Elimelech's who is very wealthy—Boaz. Even though Ruth knows nothing about Boaz, she asks Naomi for permission to glean grain in the fields and ends up in Boaz's field. She seeks grace from him.

Boaz comes from Bethlehem to check on his servants. He blesses his reapers and asks his servant who the young woman is. The servant tells him she is the Moabite who came back with Naomi and asked if she could gather the leftovers. Boaz tells Ruth she can glean only in his field and when she is thirsty, she can drink from his vessels. She is to bide close to his maidens and refuse the young men.

Ruth bows in gratefulness. She tells him she is a stranger and questions his grace. Boaz tells her that her sacrifice has not gone unnoticed. She has left her family, land, and people; therefore, she is to be rewarded for her work. He also acknowledges her trust in God. Ruth asks for favor and Boaz grants her food at mealtime, companionship beside the reapers, and permission to gather among the sheaves.

Ruth returns to Naomi with plenty of food and her mother-in-law asks her where she has gleaned. Naomi says a blessing over the one who showed her grace, and Ruth tells her it was Boaz. Naomi tells her he is near to kin. Naomi blesses God for remembering them and Ruth tells Naomi what Boaz said to her - that she is to keep close by the young men until the end of harvest. Naomi advises her to go out with the maidens and stay in his field. Ruth obeys Naomi by staying in Boaz's field.

Chapter Three – "Preparation for Redemption and Marriage"

Ruth finds out that Boaz is Naomi's near kinsman, but there is a nearer kinsman. Naomi seeks rest (security) for Ruth at Boaz's side. She instructs Ruth to wash, anoint, and put on her mantle. She is to get down to the threshing floor and wait until it is time to make herself known. When Boaz lies down, she is to mark the place where he lies and go in, uncover his feet, lay down, and he will tell her what to do.

Ruth goes down to the floor and after Boaz is full, she uncovers his feet and lies down. Boaz is startled and asks who it is. Ruth answers Boaz with, "I am your handmaid." She asks that his skirt be spread over her because he is a near kinsman. Boaz blesses Ruth and tells her that she is not to fear; that he will do what is needed. He is a near kinsman; however, there is a nearer kinsman. He tells her to wait and he will perform the part of the kinsman if the nearer kinsman does not.

Ruth lies at Boaz's feet until morning. She rises up early so no one will know she came into the floor. Boaz gives her six measures of barley and Ruth returns to Naomi. Ruth tells Naomi all that Boaz had done for her (six measures of barley given to help her and her mother-in-law). Naomi encourages Ruth to rest until she knows how things will turn out.

Chapter Four – "Redemption, Marriage, & Fruitfulness"

Boaz goes to the gate where the nearer kinsman passes. Boaz asks the nearer kinsman to sit down and invites ten elders to join them. He tells the nearer kinsman that Naomi needs to sell Elimelech's land and if he wants to purchase the land, then go ahead, but if not, Boaz will. The nearer kinsman agrees to redeem the land, but then reneges because Boaz tells him the redemption value includes Ruth, the Moabitess. The nearer kinsman does not want to ruin his inheritance.

The nearer kinsman gives Boaz the right to redeem the land and Ruth. He gives his word by plucking off his shoe and giving it to Boaz. Those who were in the gate were witnesses and gave a blessing: "The

Lord make the woman like Rachel and Leah and may the house be like that of Pharez."

Boaz takes Ruth as his wife and they conceive and bear a son. The women tell Naomi she is blessed of the Lord and that the child will restore her back to health and keep her young. Naomi takes the child and cares for him. The neighbor women call the child, Obed, who eventually becomes the father of Jesse and the grandfather of David. These are the generations: Pharez, Hezron, Ram, Amminadab, Nahshon, Salmon, Boaz, Obed, Jesse, David.

Appendix II

PUTTING IT ALL TOGETHER

Chapter One – "Famine and Death"

During the time when men did their own thing, there was hunger in Bethlehem-Judah (the House of Bread). Elimelech (God of the king - boss) takes his wife and two sons to Moab (wash pot) to provide the physical needs for his family rather than stay in the place of spiritual provision.

Elimelech dies and Naomi (pleasant), Mahlon (sickly) and Chilion (wasting away) remain in their place of spiritual decadence. The two sons marry Moabite women (non-believers), Orpah (stiff-necked) and Ruth (friendship). The sons die, so Naomi decides to return to her homeland after hearing that there is grain in "The House of Bread."

Orpah and Ruth decide to go with Naomi, but three times Naomi tries to persuade them to return to their own land, people and their families. Orpah does not want to conform, obey, or imitate the Lord. Her main reason for going back to her people was because she did not believe there was a future for her in "The House of Bread."

After a fourth appeal from Naomi to return to her homeland, Ruth will rule and reign with the Lord as she clings to Naomi and promises that she will follow her and embrace her people and her God for life.

When Naomi and Ruth approach Naomi's homeland, the women in "The House of Bread" do not even recognize Naomi because she believes her plight is a direct result of God's judgment. Naomi suffers from an identity crisis. She does not know who God is or what her purpose is. She tells the women to call her bitter because there is no hope for her.

Chapter Two – "Training Camp"

Ruth goes to the fields to gather grain for Naomi and herself with the hope that she will be shown grace (kindness) by the landowner. Ruth ends up on Boaz's (strength) property, a close relative of Elimelech. Boaz notices Ruth and asks his servant about her. The servant knows she has left a place of bondage and would like to enter into an intimate relationship with the Lord.

Boaz tells Ruth to stay in the place where she will be spiritually nourished and remain pure. She is to avoid all distractions and partake of the food that he gives her. She immediately wonders why he has shown her great favor since she is an outsider (non-Jew). Boaz tells her that it is because of her kindness shown toward Naomi (Jew), her sacrifice for leaving her family, land, and people, and her trust in the Lord.

Ruth appeals for favor and Boaz gives her permission to eat at his servants' table, and she is able to gather more than her allotted share of grain. When she returns home to Naomi, she sees how much she has gleaned and Naomi knows that God has blessed her. Not only was Ruth led to Boaz's field, but he was Elimelech's relative. Naomi gives Ruth advice to remain with Boaz's young maidens in his fields and Ruth obeys her.

Chapter Three – "Preparation for Redemption and Marriage"

Naomi knows that according to the Levirate law, Boaz can redeem the family property and Ruth, so she seeks a secure future for Ruth. She encourages her to prepare herself and make herself known to Boaz. God wants us to know Him and be known by Him. Ruth is told to wash (cleansing by the Word – water baptism), anoint (Holy Spirit baptism), and clothe herself (put on Christ), and go to the threshing floor (death to the flesh) where Boaz lies. She is to go in (partake of His death), uncover his feet (resurrection), lie there and wait for him to tell her what she should do (live His life through her).

Ruth obeys. Boaz wakes up startled by her presence and asks who it is. Ruth asks him to spread his skirt (she wants to identify with Him fully) over his handmaiden because he is a near kinsman. Boaz blesses her because she has not pursued her own needs. He tells her not to fear because he is going to do what is required—as she is known by the city as a virtuous woman. (God wants a pure bride.)

Boaz proceeds to tell Ruth there is a nearer kinsman (the law) than he. She is to wait and he will make sure she is redeemed (restored to the original state). She rises up early and Boaz gives her six (the measure of man) measures of barley and she returns to Naomi—a sign of Boaz's intentions to take care of Ruth. Naomi asks her how it went. Naomi reassures Ruth that Boaz will take care of her that day.

Chapter Four – "Redemption, Marriage, & Fruitfulness"

Boaz (Jesus) goes to the marketplace (the place of judgment) and waits until he sees the nearer kinsman (the law) and asks him to sit down. Jesus fulfills the law. Boaz asks ten (number for a witness) men of the elders to join them. He tells the nearer kinsman about Naomi's need to sell Elimelech's land. The nearer kinsman agrees to buy the land until he learns that he must also take Ruth, the Moabitess (only Jesus can redeem man as the law only points man to God). The nearer kinsman would not endanger his own inheritance, so he gives Boaz the right to be her kinsman redeemer. To confirm this, the nearer kinsman takes off his shoe (God's path, not men's) and gives it to Boaz in front of the ten witnesses.

The elders affirm the covenant (promise) and speak blessings over Ruth, that she would be fruitful in the kingdom of God, keeping the bloodline pure. Boaz takes Ruth as his wife and she conceives and bears a son. The women tell Naomi she is blessed with a kinsman redeemer who restores life and sustains old age and with Ruth, who loves Naomi and bears a son in the lineage of David and Jesus. Naomi takes the child (at this point, I wonder if this is prophetic of the church being taken up and of the Jews knowing their Messiah because Naomi, not Ruth, nurses the child.) and cares for him. The neighbor women call him "Servant."

ENDNOTES

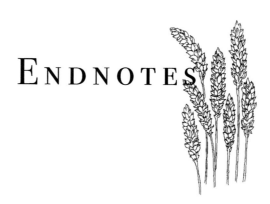

Dedication

1. James Strong, S.T.D., LL.D, *The Exhaustive Concordance of the Bible* (Peabody, Massachusetts, Hendrickson Publishers), 51.

2. James Strong, S.T.D., LL.D, *The Exhaustive Concordance of the Bible* (Peabody, Massachusetts, Hendrickson Publishers), 76.

Chapter Two

3. James Strong, S.T.D., LL.D, *The Exhaustive Concordance of the Bible* (Peabody, Massachusetts, Hendrickson Publishers), 58.

4. *Merriam Webster's Collegiate Dictionary Tenth Edition* (Springfield, Massachusetts, Merriam Webster, 1993), 567.

Chapter Three

5. James Strong, S.T.D., LL.D, *The Exhaustive Concordance of the Bible* (Peabody, Massachusetts, Hendrickson Publishers), 13.

6. James Strong, S.T.D., LL.D, *The Exhaustive Concordance of the Bible* (Peabody, Massachusetts, Hendrickson Publishers), 47.

7. James Strong, S.T.D., LL.D, *The Exhaustive Concordance of the Bible* (Peabody, Massachusetts, Hendrickson Publishers), 9, 42, 50 & 62.

Chapter Four

8. Wikipedia, http://en.wikipedia.org/wiki/literary_devices (accessed December 22, 2008).

9. *King James Easy-Reading Study Bible* (Goodyear, AZ, G.E.M. Publishing, 2002), 427-432.

10. James Strong, S.T.D., LL.D, *The Exhaustive Concordance of the Bible* (Peabody, Massachusetts, Hendrickson Publishers), 64.

Chapter Nine

11. James Strong, S.T.D., LL.D, *The Exhaustive Concordance of the Bible* (Peabody, Massachusetts, Hendrickson Publishers), 75, 30, 71, 12 & 43.

12. James Strong, S.T.D., LL.D, *The Exhaustive Concordance of the Bible* (Peabody, Massachusetts, Hendrickson Publishers), 108, 82, 118, 28, 12, 122, 115, 27, 71 & 76.

13. James Strong, S.T.D., LL.D, *The Exhaustive Concordance of the Bible* (Peabody, Massachusetts, Hendrickson Publishers), 109, 62, 20, 13, 79, 64, 55, 92, 107 & 71.

14. *King James Easy-Reading Study Bible* (Goodyear, AZ, G.E.M. Publishing, 2002), 773.

15. Ira Milligan, *Understanding the Dreams You Dream* (Shippensburg, PA, Destiny Image Publishers, 1997), 92.

16. James Strong, S.T.D., LL.D, *The Exhaustive Concordance of the Bible* (Peabody, Massachusetts, Hendrickson Publishers), 82 & 108.

17. Merrill F. Unger, *The New Unger's Bible Dictionary* (Chicago, IL, Moody Press, 1988), 723-724.

18. Merrill F. Unger, *The New Unger's Bible Dictionary* (Chicago, IL, Moody Press, 1988), 719-720.

19. James Strong, S.T.D., LL.D, *The Exhaustive Concordance of the Bible* (Peabody, Massachusetts, Hendrickson Publishers), 26.

20. Merrill F. Unger, *The New Unger's Bible Dictionary* (Chicago, IL, Moody Press, 1988), 1328.

21. Merrill F. Unger, *The New Unger's Bible Dictionary* (Chicago, IL, Moody Press, 1988), 400.

22. Merrill F. Unger, *The New Unger's Bible Dictionary* (Chicago, IL, Moody Press, 1988), 817-818.

23. James Strong, S.T.D., LL.D, *The Exhaustive Concordance of the Bible* (Peabody, Massachusetts, Hendrickson Publishers), 25, 41, 89, 78, 8, 117, 112 & 79.

24. James Strong, S.T.D., LL.D, *The Exhaustive Concordance of the Bible* (Peabody, Massachusetts, Hendrickson Publishers), 41 & 56.

25. Merrill F. Unger, *The New Unger's Bible Dictionary* (Chicago, IL, Moody Press, 1988), 742.

26. Merrill F. Unger, *The New Unger's Bible Dictionary* (Chicago, IL, Moody Press, 1988), 35-36.

27. Merrill F. Unger, *The New Unger's Bible Dictionary* (Chicago, IL, Moody Press, 1988), 842.

28. James Strong, S.T.D., LL.D, *The Exhaustive Concordance of the Bible* (Peabody, Massachusetts, Hendrickson Publishers), 68, 120, 108, 82, 47 & 39.

29. Merrill F. Unger, *The New Unger's Bible Dictionary* (Chicago, IL, Moody Press, 1988), 318-324, 438, 817-820 & 1277.

30. Merrill F. Unger, *The New Unger's Bible Dictionary* (Chicago, IL, Moody Press, 1988), 1277.

31. Merrill F. Unger, *The New Unger's Bible Dictionary* (Chicago, IL, Moody Press, 1988), 1277 & 35-36.

32. James Strong, S.T.D., LL.D, *The Exhaustive Concordance of the Bible* (Peabody, Massachusetts, Hendrickson Publishers), 122 & 12 and Merrill F. Unger, The New Unger's Bible Dictionary (Chicago, IL, Moody Press, 1988), 842.

33. James Strong, S.T.D., LL.D, *The Exhaustive Concordance of the Bible* (Peabody, Massachusetts, Hendrickson Publishers), 119, 25, 115, 85, 104, 113 & 54.

34. Ira Milligan, *Understanding the Dreams You Dream* (Shippensburg, PA, Destiny Image Publishers, 1997), 93.

35. James Strong, S.T.D., LL.D, *The Exhaustive Concordance of the Bible* (Peabody, Massachusetts, Hendrickson Publishers), 21-22.

36. Ira Milligan, *Understanding the Dreams You Dream* (Shippensburg, PA, Destiny Image Publishers, 1997), 95.

AVAILABLE FOR SPEAKING ENGAGEMENTS

Terri Lustig (http://terrilustig.authorweblog.com/ or 513-783-7723) is prepared to speak on various topics for women's retreats, Bible conferences, home groups, churches, Pregnancy Care Centers, Teen Challenge groups, and home school conventions. Some of her themes include: *Famine: Fight or Flight, Taking the Narrow Road, God's Fingerprints, The Power of the Spoken Word, Ripe for God's Blessings, Leaving a Legacy of Love, Hearkening to the Voice of the Lord, Lying at His Feet, Experiencing an Identity Crisis, Who's to Blame?, Where is God When Life Stinks?,* and much more.